nothing can stop
YOU

nothing can stop

YOU

a revolutionary guide to
Unleash Your Authentic Self

ERIN RACHEL DOPPELT

HAMPTON ROADS

This edition first published in 2024 by Hampton Roads Publishing, an imprint of
Red Wheel/Weiser, LLC
With offices at:
65 Parker Street, Suite 7
Newburyport, MA 01950
Sign up for our newsletter and special offers by going to
www.redwheelweiser.com/newsletter

Cover design by Sky Peck Design
Interior design by Brittany Craig, images by iStock.com
Typeset in Arno Pro

Library of Congress Cataloging-in-Publication Data

Names: Doppelt, Erin Rachel, author.
Title: Nothing can stop you : a revolutionary guide to unleash your authentic self / Erin Rachel Doppelt.
Description: Newburyport, MA : Hampton Roads, 2024. | Includes bibliographical references. | Summary: "A self-study book that blends Eastern ritual and Western psychology, this is a hands-on guide for self-reflection. What is your deepest desire and dream? Answering that question means committing to your own journey, becoming an active participant in your own life, and showing up for your most authentic Self"-- Provided by publisher.
Identifiers: LCCN 2023050144 | ISBN 9781642970500 (trade paperback) | ISBN 9781612834894 (ebook) Subjects: LCSH: Self-realization. | Self-realization--Religious aspects. | Mind and body. | BISAC: BODY, MIND & SPIRIT / Inspiration & Personal Growth | SELF-HELP / Spiritual
Classification: LCC BF637.S4 .D667 2024 | DDC 158.1--dc23/eng/20231205
LC record available at https://lccn.loc.gov/2023050144

Printed in the United States of America
IBI

10 9 8 7 6 5 4 3 2 1

To my parents, for always leaving the hall light on.
I love you from the top of my head to the tips of my toes,
and with all my heart.

L'chaim, l'ahava, v'tuv lev.

לחיים לאהבה וטוב לב

To life, to love, to a good heart.

contents

author's note

Some names and identifying details of clients and friends in this book have been changed in order to protect their privacy. In a few instances, I have created composites to illustrate a point.

This book is intended to provide helpful information and support that is rooted in spiritual themes and psychological frameworks. It is not meant to be used to diagnose or treat any specific medical conditions, and it is not a substitute for seeking professional help and treatment. If you know or suspect you have a medical condition, are experiencing physical symptoms, or if you feel unwell, seek your physician's advice before practicing the exercises in this book.

Readers using the information in this book do so entirely at their own risk, and the author and publisher accept no liability if adverse effects are caused.

PREFACE

liberation

I wanted more.

I was spiritually starved and had an all-consuming hunger to learn—about other cultures, food, the way people think, love, pray, and see the world.

Why is wanting more such a rebellious act?

This is what I thought as my thighs chaffed, taking one dusty step after another, my feet dragging me forward into the vast Middle Eastern desert. My family, my corporate job I'd just quit, my Chicago friends and comforts, all half a world away.

A fly landed on my hunched shoulder—impressed by my stench, I suppose. Clearly, my natural deodorant wasn't working. I paused, catching my breath, noticing I was in fact far away from the ashram I was staying in, just a speck of dust in this never-ending desert.

What am I doing? was the main thought on repeat. I'd landed in Israel a few weeks ago with a one-way plane ticket and no plan, just a desperate need to honor that quiet voice within to trust, show up, and pursue the adventure. My heart rate rose, my palms began to sweat, and I noticed a little crater to my right and laid down to slow my soon-to-be full-blown panic attack.

I sank deeper into the crater, allowing the edge to provide just enough shade to shield my eyes from the sun. *How can I do this work if my biggest obstacle is me? If, in my core, I don't feel worthy to pursue this path? What even is this path?* I judged myself so deeply for desiring "more." *I need guidance. I need help.* I closed my eyes. Tears poured down my face. My body shivered. A light filled every cell in my body. A voice with utter clarity and alignment spoke to me from within: *You're never alone,* it said. *You're being guided. Pursue your deepest dreams. I am here with you.*

I opened my eyes, stood up, and walked back to the ashram.

INTRODUCTION

do you have an open mind?

Are you down for the deep work?

Do you desire to live on your highest possible timeline?

You are responsible for your deepest desires and dreams. I know this because in my early adult life, I realized no one was coming to save me. No one was going to open my journals and read all the dreams I'd once had for myself. The Pinterest boards, vision planners, and daydreaming thoughts hung out in the ether, in the space between where I was and where I desperately desired to be. But I knew I had to do the work because no one was going to hand me my dreams on a silver platter. You have to show up and do the work. Herein lies the medicine of this book. Nothing can stop you from pursuing your heart's desires.

As we embark on this journey together, it's important that you know you are welcome here. A million events had to occur for this book to land in your hands. It is not an accident for you to be experiencing this book right now; and for that

I am grateful. Take a deep breath with me, because this book is infused with my highest wish for all:

- ✻ That you show up for Self, your desires, and your deepest dreams;

- ✻ That you are gentle with Self;

- ✻ That you pursue your dreams while staying connected to your wise inner teacher; and

- ✻ That you create a wonderful life for Self that's rooted in alignment.

It is your birthright to live your own life. In these pages, I share some of my own stories that led me to deepen my connection to my inner Self. Pulled from these stories are frameworks, exercises, and rituals rooted in both Eastern ritual and Western psychology that will guide you as you deepen your own connection to yourself, leading you to your most joyful, creative life. This path stems from grounded decision-making, honoring thyself and doing the work needed to change any beliefs that are limiting, untrue, and keeping you in the state of inaction on your desires. This will guide you to your "highest possible timeline," the best path for your soul-authentic Self, the truest version of you.

WHAT YOU'LL DISCOVER

In this book, I'm going to show you how to tune in to who you truly are and create a life that's meaningful, joyful, and nourishing. Some of this work will be challenging—we're going to get quiet, look inward, and face some maybe awkward, maybe painful, hard truths about ourselves. But I promise this will all pay off in the long run, in the form of nurturing meaningful relationships that sustain us; and in pursuing goals that align with our true path. My mission is to support you to "do the thing," honoring the actual desires deep in your soul. Through a progression of rituals, embodiment practices, and meditations we'll get to the core of what actually fills you up, what makes you uniquely happy and content. We are going to illuminate your authentic Self and instill deep confidence and trust in your ability to make the decisions that are right for you.

This work is open to everyone, and it doesn't require you to buy anything to get started. But I would, however, recommend getting a notebook to record your answers to the prompts and to jot down other thoughts as you're reading. Alternatively, you could just type out your responses into the Notes app on your phone. There are benefits to writing things out longhand, but I'm also acutely aware of how much faster it is to type or leave yourself a voice memo. So do what works best for you. We're going to cover quite a bit of ground, so here's a quick overview of what to expect:

In Chapter 1, we're going to show up for ourselves. This is the crucial first step. I share with you how anxiety became one of my biggest teachers to guiding me toward the spiritual path. You will be introduced to the life-altering (and mandatory) practice of Mornings with Meaning and learn about honoring your inner child.

In Chapter 2, I share with you a pivotal story in my life where I met a false guru while staying at an Ayurvedic ashram in Northern India. We then explore different meditation practices to regulate the nervous system and see how important it is to have agency to leave an uncomfy situation.

Chapter 3 focuses on staying strong when we're challenged and face outside pressure—whether that's to conform, to acquiesce, or to play it small so others can feel more comfortable. I share with you an experience I had during my yoga teacher training in Southern India and how gratitude is one of my pathways to the sacred.

In Chapter 4, we'll explore the science of happiness and how to implement daily practices that will help you to live your happiest, most meaningful life.

Chapter 5 is all about emotional intelligence, the spiritual practice of slowing down and defining the major beliefs that govern your life.

Chapter 6 is one of my most cherished stories of all, the details on how I manifested my husband and how you can use manifestation to call in your dreams too. This chapter features the powerful practice of Snapshot Manifestation.

In Chapter 7, we'll tackle two of the most common roadblocks to achieving our goals: perfectionism and procrastination. We'll learn what's at the root of them and how to stay motivated and moving.

I believe that exploring the spiritual side of ourselves is an essential part of unlocking our true selves, and so I've devoted all of Chapter 8 to deepening and questioning our relationships to God, or a higher power as you understand it. And throughout this book, I encourage you to foster your connection with your inner Self as well as your relationship with a higher power. This chapter highlights the innate ability for children to be spiritual and how we can nurture that for future generations.

In Chapter 9, we discuss the concept of legacy energy—that is, how you want to leave this world. We will also explore what makes life meaningful and learn about the law of massive aligned action (LMAA) and what it means to be the beneficial presence (BP).

Chapter 10 is about exploring our language of Self and reframing practices to shift toward a more positive and uplifting mindset. This chapter also highlights common phrases we say in our English-speaking culture that may contribute to a collective limiting belief.

Something I've come across in my work with many, many people is how chronically undernourished we are. What I mean is that given all the myriad demands on our time, and the stress this causes, giving our bodies what we need to grow and heal and thrive is often put on the back burner. In Chapter

11, I offer a gentle reminder of some simple ways to make sure we are nourishing our bodies and our souls every day.

Chapter 12 dives into the cyclical nature of everything, and offers some ways to celebrate and harness the power of these cycles for our benefit.

Finally, Chapter 13 is an invitation to go forth and share your wonderful, imperfect, passionate, aligned, authentic Self with others by creating a powerful gathering—and encouraging others to explore their own authentic selves with you. Our growth is never done, and we're all always going to be changing. What better way to move into the next phase on your path than with the community of others?

I designed this book for you to read cover to cover first, so you can see how concepts build on one another. However, each chapter can stand alone, so you can return to chapters at random as you need them. In every chapter you will find actionable rituals and exercises to help you start putting these principles into practice right away. Also, some spiritual themes, key terms, and psychological concepts are purposefully repeated to encourage you to integrate the ideas in multiple ways. Once you've read the book, answered the questions, and done the rituals and meditations, I encourage you to revisit this material as a mindful check-in.

LET'S GET STARTED

So happy to have you here!

When I meet someone who wants it all—the connection to spirit, the abundance, the adventure, the romance, the health and vitality—I share this with them: *You have to do the work. No one can do it for you.* This is an intimate relationship between you and your own obstacles, and now is a superb time to show up. You are your own best friend and biggest cheerleader, or you are the bully in your story who keeps you playing small. On this journey, as you do the work, your connection to yourself will deepen and will light your path.

Now is the time to release judgment and make a pact with your inner Self. This is your time to shine. May you show up for yourself every day in every way. May the practices in this book deepen your connection to yourself and the world. And remember, when moving through life connected to your inner wisdom and most authentic Self,

nothing can stop you.

CHAPTER 1

breathe in,
show up

I do my thing, and you do your thing.
I am not in this world to live up to your expectations.
And you are not in this world to live up to mine.
You are you and I am I,
And if by chance we find each other,
It's beautiful.
If not, it can't be helped.

—FREDERICK S. PERLS, GESTALT THERAPY VERBATIM

This is not what you intended, I told myself. I remember thinking, *Wow, how did this become my life? How did I end up in this ashram with a Holocaust denier? Why is this guru trying to fuck me? Why am I trusting this shaman, who claims he can predict the future, more than I am trusting myself?*

It leads to the work of tuning inward.

"Know thyself."

This maxim appears at the entrance of the Temple of Apollo at Delphi, where over twenty-five hundred years ago, the Greek oracle Pythia communed with the spirit world. Its wisdom holds true even today.

Who are you, really? How did you become this way? And what steps must you take to become the most authentic version of yourself (aka the person you were always meant to be)? These are some of the big questions we'll be exploring in this book.

When you know who you are, you are dangerous. You are not easily manipulated, and you know what is meant for your soul. You have a strong sense of self, clarity on who you are and on how you want to show up—day in and day out. You can say yes or no to decisions easily because your inner knowing guides you. The sooner you like who you are, and the sooner you are happy with yourself, the more miraculous life will be.

So often my clients come to me exhausted by all the self-development options. My one client Andy comes to mind. She knew that going to yoga after work instead of happy hour was better for her mental health, but it took so much effort to decline a drink and pull out the yoga mat. Andy knew that waking up, getting out of bed, and perhaps journaling or breathing a bit before work would feel nourishing, but instead she opens up her phone and scrolls. She desires to be in a romantic relationship but cannot muster up the stamina or confidence to get back on the dating apps or ask for an introduction. Her fridge is full of

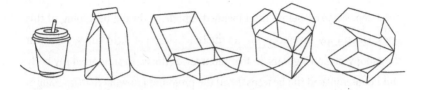

fresh foods, yet the exhaustion of the day always leaves Andy ordering in. This cycle continues, leading to nights of insomnia, moments of extreme anxiety, and a deep belief system that there has to be something more—and perhaps even a question around, *Am I deserving to have more?* And it's not that she doesn't enjoy her life—she has a nice couple of friends, a job that brings her some sense of accomplishment, and social events that she looks forward to. She just feels underwhelmed by it all. She thinks there has to be a better way. She wanted more for herself.

Andy is an example of someone who moves through the day doing mundane tasks that remind her, "This isn't what I wanted for myself. This isn't the life I dreamed of when I was younger." Instead of judging or ignoring this inner voice—this higher self-knowing—we can lean in and use this as our true north navigation system.

If you yearn to live life out loud and show up for your deepest desires and dreams, now is the time to deepen your connection to your inner Self. In fact, this is your greatest work. It's time to show up and claim (or reclaim) your life. A side effect of honoring your inner Self is waking up to why you are the way you are and to the miracles all around you—and awakening to the truth of what needs to shift so you can live your authentic, nourished life.

What does it take to wake up and show up for ourselves in this modern world? It starts with making some space and getting quiet.

MAKING SPACE

Years ago, six years before the Liberated experience in the beginning of this book, when I was seventeen, I lay in the Israeli desert at night and stared up at the canopy of glowing stars. In that moment, as the earth supported my body and I contemplated the heavens, I had the profound knowing that anything is possible. A strong feeling of awe washed over me. While a rendition of Leonard Cohen's "Hallelujah" played in the background, I experienced peace in my body. I loved the nourishing feeling of connecting to myself, and I felt the stars witness my subtle inner transformation. The stars above me reflected what I learned to be true in that moment: that I can shine. A small voice whispered, *Erin, your calling in the world is to share this feeling of nourishment, to remember that anything is possible, and to support others to shine as well, in their own way, just like these stars.*

This inner voice, or *knowing*, wasn't something people around me talked about. My academic curriculum did not nurture it. Some people call it a gut feeling; others call it intuition. It felt like a higher, happier, more authentic version of myself was trying to break through and communicate with me. I called her my "inner guru." At the time I was not yet a yogi, but I heard this term thrown around in yoga studios, philosophy books, and even at my synagogue.

Years later, while studying at Columbia University, the core curriculum focused on listening to our inner instrument of knowing, truth, and direction. Science, spirituality, and psychology converged. I was fascinated and elated to discover that researchers and educators had been working on formal language and frameworks to understand the feeling I had stumbled upon in the desert as a teenager. Now, I could finally explain how my intuition had guided me to make the decisions I'd made up to this point—and I could teach others how to access this latent superpower for themselves.

My inner guru was present during my sorority girl days. As I partied, it whispered in my ear that my undergraduate degree, my social group, even the way I dressed, were all out of alignment. It reminded me daily (usually in the middle of the night) that I was not happy; I was not connected to the best version of myself. Amidst it all—the themed mixers, the dating, the late-night binge eating, the unkind gossip—anxiety rocked my world and took some of my shine. I cried at all hours of the day, overate to self-soothe, and suffered through sleepless night after sleepless night. In desperation, I lay prostrate on my dorm room carpet and surrendered. I prayed. For a different headspace. For clarity. To feel better. I prayed to God as I understood it, to all my ancestors, and to all those who watch over me. *Help me. I don't want to feel like this anymore!* The wisdom I received changed my life. The inner voice I heard was a quiet, clear, stern reminder: *Pause. Listen to your inner guru. Come back home to yourself.*

So, I did. It was easier because I was exhausted. I had nothing to lose. I listened, breathed, and tuned inward. Everything changed. My spiritual connection and my relationship to Self transformed. I began binge-reading books in the self-help section, spending more time alone, and drinking more water. My self-paced studies escalated to yoga classes, breathwork sessions, and guided meditations on YouTube. I feasted on free spiritual content online. Girls from my sorority began meditating with me in my dorm room. That's when I became a way-shower. Curious about yogic lineage, I promised myself that I would get to India one day. Remembering how connected I'd felt to myself in the Israeli desert at seventeen, I vowed to explore Israel, too. My spiritual exploration in my dorm room helped me build a foundation for what I truly desired. I was hungry for my unedited Self. I wanted to experience and know the fullest embodiment of me.

After college I worked in corporate marketing for a health food brand. Even though I enjoyed most parts of my job, it left me overworked and feeling less connected to myself. When I woke up on weekend mornings, I felt like I had a hole in my heart. I was almost a year out of college, and I longed for adventure, creativity, and a nourishing spiritual life. But my inner guru got shoved down between bites of late-night beef sandwiches (while I was trying to be vegan), cast aside during happy-hour cocktails that left me anxious, and pushed away during horrid bouts of insomnia. But no matter what, thankfully, my inner guru kept trying to reconnect.

In the thick of the Chicago winter, I went on a horrible first date. He took me for pizza, we drank red wine, and he seemed like a nice guy. But he wasn't my guy, and I wasn't in the right headspace to even be there. My depressive winter blues weighed down the conversation. I excused myself to use the restroom, opened my phone, and saw a bolded rejection letter from a fellowship I'd applied to in Israel. I sat down on the toilet seat and sobbed. I didn't want to be this person. I had so much to be grateful for and felt guilty that I couldn't just appreciate it. But my inner guru kept reminding me, *This is not your highest possible timeline. You are more than allowed to desire a different path.*

When I woke up the next morning, all I could think was, I am not a match for this. I had big dreams and desires, and yet here I was ... hungover, in a mouse-infested apartment, feeling like a stranger to myself. It was scary. As a teen, I'd been sold on the idea that being an adult was interesting and exciting; now, as a new adult, all I felt was out of alignment. I didn't want to appear ungrateful because there was a part of me that wanted the "marketing professional corporate America" job experience. But I couldn't help but feel like the movies made it look much more fabulous than it really was. Wasn't I allowed to want more?

I was the only person in my social circle interested in living a spiritual life. I was obsessed with yoga, meditation, journaling, self-improvement, and seeking joyful moments, but I was alone on the journey. The concept of pursuing travel and leaving everything behind to explore the world scared me to my core, but anything was better than waking up to this . . . hollowness, disconnection, undernourishment. I promised myself I would go for it. I would follow my dreams because no one else was going to do it for me. I couldn't let myself down.

So, I did what everyone around me called "bananas." I quit my marketing job, moved back into my parents' house, continued saving most of my money, and made a pact with my inner guru. I'd show up for myself, take up space in this lifetime, and take aligned action. My inner guru would keep me on track and help me do my soul work and live my life authentically. This led to me saying yes to leading a trip to Israel—an opportunity I was a perfect fit for, as I'd been guiding summer teen tours to Israel the previous years—and I stayed there. I booked plane tickets to India and Bali, applied to a master's degree program I believed was out of my reach, and explored exciting places in between.

So, my friend, what about you? Are you living a life you love? Is this what you intended? You have always known—or at least had glimpses—of what you truly desire and what you crave in life. These moments may have occurred when you were younger and unaware of the obstacles that would arise in your future. Maybe it's a whisper that escapes from your lips in the middle of the night, offering insight into a troubling relationship. Or it's an out-of-the-blue idea that just appears when you wake up one morning. Maybe it's awakening to an inner conflict while walking yourself home after another underwhelming first date (or after hanging out with friends who leave you feeling depleted). Perhaps, on your way home, you walk down a different street and find yourself surrounded by beautiful lights that speak to your soul and help you feel light. Maybe your job, your day-to-day activities, a stressful family member, or a person in your life reminds you of how far away you are from living the life you've dreamed about . . . and then you find a book on a shelf that you know was meant for you.

Realizing you have disconnected from aspects of your life that once inspired or motivated you is all part of the journey—and so is noticing the tiny moments of rightness, those small reminders of what it feels like to be aligned with the things that make your soul swoon. As your inner Self tries to contact you and takes up more space in your life, you are also tapping into what it is like to feel joy in the present moment. Like when you have your morning cup of tea or coffee and realize that you feel comfy cozy in your body. Or you hear a song that brings back a joyful, nourishing memory. Perhaps it's when you are curious, creative, or invested in something bigger than yourself, thriving in your love of learning. Maybe it's even a time when you feel seen in a loving relationship—or just seen for who you truly are at your core.

Over time, these moments add up. They signify what is working in your life and what moments or events are connected to your true Self. This is part of the journey of being *soul authentic,* allowing yourself to live out loud.

MORNINGS WITH MEANING

There is one golden guideline in the process I call "becoming soul-authentic and strengthening your inner guru connection." Starting today, every morning, you will have a Morning with Meaning. *This practice is mandatory.* In the mornings, when you're in your authentic energy, you can move into this flexible ritual. It feels so good. It's a time to breathe and live in the present moment. It's a time for you to honor yourself.

A Morning with Meaning is not a one-size-fits-all model. What works for you is likely to differ from what works for your loved ones or friends. A Morning with Meaning is at least eighteen minutes, a digestible amount of time for both beginners and experts. In many cultures, the number eighteen is symbolic. In Judaism, for example, eighteen is the numeric value of *chai* (חי), which means "life" in Hebrew. In many cultures, age eighteen represents increased independence. TED Talks are frequently about eighteen minutes long, as it is enough time to teach a new skill or help an audience understand a concept while keeping their attention. So, make your Mornings with Meaning a minimum of eighteen minutes to enjoy the maximum benefit.

If you absolutely cannot make time in the morning (say, if you have to get little ones off to school or daycare and every second is jam-packed from the moment you wake up), try to adapt this practice to start as early as you possibly can. Maybe lunchtime is your first opportunity. Maybe it's an afternoon coffee break. First thing in the morning is best; but sometime is better than never. You can also break this practice up into nine minutes here and nine minutes later in the day. That said, let's talk about what the ideal Morning with Meaning looks like.

When we honor a Morning with Meaning, we tell ourselves and the world, "I'm expanding. I'm taking up space in this life." This is living with intention and being an active participant in your life. This is nourishment for the soul and life force energy.

When you dedicate time to this practice every morning, energy and intention will follow you into your day. Little by little, you're strengthening your connection to your inner wisdom. And the cumulative effect has the power to transform your life—because how we spend our days is how we spend our lives.

What does a Morning with Meaning entail? It's simply doing something nourishing, enjoyable, and engaging each morning. This is a flexible and infinitely adaptable practice. For example, you can try any of the following activities:

- ❋ Write in your journal

- ❋ Meditate

- ❋ Stretch

- ❋ Breathe in silence

- ✸ Go for a walk

- ✸ Cut vegetables for a stew

- ✸ Make coffee

- ✸ Dance to your favorite songs

- ✸ Garden

- ✸ Dream

- ✸ Read

- ✸ Make love with your partner or yourself

- ✸ Listen to music

- ✸ Watch clouds float by

- ✸ Lie in bed and breathe

- ✸ Draw or color in a sketchbook

- ✸ Dive into one or two of the spiritual practices in this book

You have the freedom to choose. Instead of thinking about Mornings with Meaning as a "rule," think of it more as a soulful decree to live by. One of my clients practiced slow breathing while breastfeeding her son. Another journaled about her dreams and then took a slow shower. A good friend pulls cards from her tarot deck each morning and then walks her dog while practicing a walking meditation. I travel often, so my Mornings with Meaning vary based on where I am in the world and who is there with me.

If you lose the morning and are hard on yourself for missing a practice, you can still make time for your routine in the afternoon or evening. Be kind to yourself. Give yourself a break. Take a deep breath, pause, and be gentle. Can you still fit in some time with yourself today?

If you are judging yourself, you've missed the point of Mornings with Meaning (and my intention for this book). So, before you turn this page, take a moment and ask yourself how you will begin your next few Mornings with Meaning.

JOURNAL PROMPT

Planning Your Mornings with Meaning

How will I begin my next few Mornings with Meaning?

GETTING QUIET

You have always known how you want to live this life, but sometimes you forget or get distracted. Sometimes life takes you in a direction and throws you into a whirlwind—and it's not always bad. In fact, now and then, it's wonderful, positive, and fun. Regardless, it wasn't what you intended. It wasn't what was on your heart when you dreamed of the infinite possibilities for your life. That's okay, love. Be gentle with yourself. This is where the journey begins.

We start here.
We start open.
We start honest.

We start with you, showing up for you, and strengthening your connection to yourself.

My clients frequently feel guilty for wanting more in their lives. Somewhere along the way we were conditioned to appreciate what we have and move on. But (and it's a big but) I want to give you permission to pursue more. Usually that means more time spent lying in the sun, lower-belly laughing with friends; eating food so delicious you feel it in your womb; having deep conversations with like-minded people; swimming naked in the sea; and dancing under the stars. So many of us are spiritually starved for more of these experiences. These are the moments and the emotions that awaken us to the fullness of this life.

So, what is it you want? A different path? A broader path, with more freedom, adventure, spirituality, and play? Maybe what you desire doesn't have specific language, yet you know how you want to feel. Now is a wonderful, important time to get clear on the feeling-state. It's time to pause and reflect and see what surfaces.

EMBODIMENT EXERCISE: EYE GAZING

Whenever I have a client who doesn't know how they feel about what's happening in their life (which happens more than you'd think!), I ask them to look at their eyes as I guide them through this healing practice.

To start, go to a mirror or turn on your phone's camera in selfie mode. Now look at your eyes. Notice your eye color and the whites of your eyes. Maybe there are red lines there, hinting at too much screentime. Just notice and breathe.

Pretend you're observing your eyes from when you were eleven years old. What would your eleven-year-old Self feel and think about your life and how you're living it? Would they be happy, proud, excited, anxious, sad?

Keep looking at your eyes, focusing on slow inhales and exhales. Breathe into your lower belly, allowing your stomach to press against your waistband. Exhale audibly.

Now, look at your eyes again. You're in the present moment. What do those eyes tell you about your life? Those eyes see your world daily. Pause for a moment and reflect. Notice how you feel and breathe here for a couple minutes.

On your next inhale, look into your eyes again and imagine those eyes looking back at you in the mirror when you're eighty. Pause for a moment and reflect. Notice what feelings come up for you and breathe here for a minute or two. How does it feel to connect to different versions of yourself?

THE SOUND OF SILENCE

The Simon and Garfunkel live at Madison Square Garden record played while I sat on the couch, staring out the window up at the blue sky. I sipped on my black coffee, an Arabic earthy blend that I'd made a few minutes earlier. Lentils laid out in the sunshine began to sprout. I sang along with the record and pulled out my journal, moving between a gentle sway meditation and quietly jotting down the dreams I'd had the night before.

I was staying in a one-bedroom apartment in the Ramat Gan neighborhood outside Tel Aviv, Israel. The couple who owned the apartment were on their honeymoon, and through a Facebook group connection I'd rented their place for six weeks. The main wall was all sliding doors and overlooked a busy street, where I could happily people watch all day. I opened the whole side of the house and basked in the sunshine while moving into my Morning with Meaning. This was my time to "Account for my Soul," take time with myself, relearn who I was at my core, and regulate my nervous system.

That apartment became my cocoon. I was truly alone for the first time in my life. I had no roommates, no boss to answer to. My family was on the other side of the world, and I felt free—to sleep as late as I wanted, to eat however I desired, and to dictate my schedule. I wore loose, hippie style muumuus and took long walks through different neighborhoods, listening to the sound of my heartbeat and the rhythm of my breath. I daydreamed and romanticized all the things I desired. Before the sun set around 5:30 p.m., I often walked ninety minutes into Tel Aviv to meet friends for dinner when I desired to leave my solo cocoon and socialize. I started writing parts of this book, jotting down my thoughts and feelings, things I wished I'd known in college, and my hopes for the future. *What would it look and feel like?* I had space to be quiet, to reflect, to relax into silence, and to be with myself. It was life-changing. There are positives and negatives about silence.

The positive is that if you are overstimulated (which can be defined as doing too many things that don't nourish you), it's time for peace. It's time for stillness. However, silence also means you are confronting yourself: your past, your emotions, anything you have avoided in your life. You cannot hide from silence.

Many people fear silence. It's why we fill our schedules to the brim, distract ourselves with Netflix, overeat, scroll endlessly on social media, or have that 5:00 p.m. glass of wine. These are coping strategies we have normalized in society to avoid unprocessed emotions. When you take time to be in your own presence, you meet the emotions you have avoided your whole life. This can be powerful for those on the spiritual path and may be paired with an emotional breakthrough or a moment of healing.

Honoring your most authentic Self is of the highest priority on your spiritual journey. Otherwise, you may find yourself following a formula that doesn't nourish you. On my spiritual journey, I felt like it was mandatory for me to spend a significant amount of time in silence, not realizing or honoring at the time that I find God, connection to a higher presence, in connection with others. Human connection and conversation are the most nourishing, fulfilling moments in my life. After trying lots of different approaches, I found that partial silence feels great to me—especially during pre-bed hours, in the early mornings, and at mealtime. I encourage you to try out an intentional silence practice and take note of how it makes you feel. You'll find what works best for you, too.

EMBODIMENT PRACTICE: WORK WITH SILENCE

If you're feeling overstimulated and are called to a quieter life, try being silent in your home from 9:00 p.m. to 9:00 a.m. Turn off the Wi-Fi, dim the lights, and light incense to shift from your usual home vibe to a sacred *shala* vibe. (*Shala* means "home" in Sanskrit.) The energy will follow. Do this solo or ask those you live with to honor this for a week and see how it feels. Please keep in mind that this means no sound of any kind—no podcasts, TV, or music—from 9:00 p.m. to 9:00 a.m. Journal about your experience afterward. Does it feel like a nervous system reset? How do you feel different? How do you feel the same? Give yourself permission to edit the duration of your silent practice to whatever feels best for you.

EMBODIMENT PRACTICE:
GETAWAY RETREAT

If you desire the next level of silence, I recommend trying a getaway. It can be luxurious, like in a nice rental home in the woods or in a landscape you love. Or you could go camping solo or with someone who is also committed to silence. Start with twenty-four to forty-eight hours and see how that feels.

Please keep in mind that silence is the focus of the getaway, not the side effect. For example, let's say you have a writing deadline and you decide to book a hotel for two nights to get as much writing done as possible. You write for two days, and a side effect was that you were alone and therefore also silent because by default there was no one to whom you could talk. The goal here was the writing and meeting your deadline, not the silence.

A true silent retreat might incorporate nature walks, yoga, meditation, and light reading while connecting to the sound of silence. Also, note if the major shift was the time in silence or the physical act of leaving your home and going to a more serene space. This will help guide you in knowing what will work best for your soul-authentic development over time.

EXPLORING FEELING-STATES

When I'm helping my clients set goals for themselves and sort out what it is they really want, I often focus on their aspirational feeling-state rather than on the goal itself. For example, I've had clients hit their goal of becoming wealthy only to realize that achieving this dream doesn't deliver the happiness and fulfillment they were expecting. Sure, maybe they can afford to fly first class, or buy box seat concert tickets, or wear designer clothing. But those short-term conveniences or thrills may not be in alignment with the feeling-state they originally wanted.

Upon diving in with one client who was a successful engineer at a Bay Area startup, I discovered that she didn't feel nourished, which is what she desired more than wealth. So, I advised her to become more clear on the feelings she wanted to experience day in and day out. She desired the feeling of adventure, creativity, and spontaneity. With some mentorship we made active decisions. This led her to signing up for a local pottery class to get her creative juices flowing, traveling to Costa Rica for a yoga retreat for adventure, and backpacking without a distinct plan for a couple days after to exercise feelings of spontaneity. When she came back to the Bay Area, she would spend her weekends hiking in different towns, allowing herself to get lost, enjoying the thrill of it.

On the other hand, I had another client, Joey, who came to me feeling very lost. He was extremely burnt out from his corporate job, and when I asked him what feelings he desired to feel in his day-to-day life, he was too depleted to come up with an answer. So, we shifted the conversation. I asked him, When was the last time you felt truly light, joyful, and nourished? He told me about a long weekend he'd spent at his friend's lake house a few months earlier and how calming it felt to be in nature with people who didn't talk about work all the time. He also mentioned how the focus was water sports and physical activity and not centered around drinking alcohol, like so many other social engagements. Based on these insights, we started off by editing his social circle and weaving in more relationships with people who had other interests outside of work. We also added in weekend getaways to go camping and visit natural water sources, which felt calming to him. Joey slowly started returning back to himself, while also seeking out activities in the city that didn't revolve around drinking. These little actions brought Joey back into alignment and helped him reconnect to some feelings of calm, inner peace, and connection that he hadn't experienced in a long time.

We understand some feeling-states universally—like the joy of children opening presents on Christmas morning, or the excitement you feel when a server approaches your table with a yummy meal. Other feeling-states are unique and intimate. For me, traveling and sitting in a café in a new city with a cup of coffee and a book is the epitome of bliss. So is walking on the beach with my husband, Jon, watching a sunset while sharing stories about our days or planning our next adventure. I hunger for these feelings and live my life to have more of those kinds of feeling-states. I've built my career and my life around experiencing the feeling of adventure, allowing flexibility to travel when I want to. That's an important priority for me. We all have those feelings we hold dear—and now I'm asking you, what can you do to bring more of that into your life going forward?

At our core, so many of us desire freedom—freedom to live life in accordance with our truth; freedom to pray, love, and eat in a nourishing way. For me, freedom looks like connecting with clients and family while living in gorgeous villas around the globe. It looks like articulating my boundaries, ideas, and beliefs; like financial abundance; like dressing how my body feels on any given day. But to gain freedom, you must become clear on what is holding you back and what you need to do to realize your dreams. We'll get to these important things, I promise. But first, let's dive in to our first meditation, one that will help us clarify what we used to love feeling long ago—and may still desire today.

YOUNGER SELF MEDITATION

This is a powerful meditation to connect you with a version of your inner child. If it is possible to practice in your childhood bedroom, then go for it! Otherwise, find a comfortable space and have a journal and pen nearby.

Once you arrive in your comfy space, sit down. Take a couple deep breaths. Release your expectations. Picture golden, braided roots at the base of your tailbone, moving through the floor, into the ground, and connecting to the earth's core. You are grounded, centered, and present. Feel this anchoring strongly before continuing.

Visualize a door to your right. The door is a color you love. Walk up to the door. The handle is crafted uniquely and feels warm in your hand. You know that when you walk through this door, you will be greeted by a younger version of yourself. Remaining connected to your breath, open the door and step inside.

The room is decorated in the same way your younger Self would decorate it: toys, tchotchkes, foods . . . all the things you loved.

You see your younger Self sitting on a beautiful couch (or possibly a bean-bag). Take a moment to greet yourself. Ask, "What's up? How old are you?"

Sit and connect in a way that feels comfortable to both of you. What does your younger Self have to share with you? Do you have a question for them? Perhaps they have a question for you, too. Converse with your younger Self. Find a natural flow.

Once you feel ready, give your younger Self a big hug and a warm goodbye.

Still anchored in your breath, walk back through the door and close it behind you. Come back to the room. Notice the golden, braided roots at the base of your tailbone. Breathe for a couple cycles. Once you feel you are back in your body, open your eyes. Take out your journal or phone and write down any epiphanies, findings, or ideas that come through. Do any of your younger Self's dreams still resonate? Does this younger you have a unique perspective on any issues you are debating?

How can you show up for this version of you?

JOURNAL PROMPT

Imagining Your Younger, Dreamer Self

Take a moment to consider what life events led you to where you are
today. Who were you trying to make happy along the way? Did your
younger Self have bigger dreams—dreams so big that, in a child's eyes,
they seemed reachable? The truth is that dream may still be present for
you. What if you treated those childhood dreams as a road map? What
if they could show you how to shift and get closer to alignment with
your true Self?

EMBODIMENT EXERCISE: SCHEDULE ALIGNMENT

Divide a piece of paper in two by drawing a vertical line down the middle. In the
left column, write all your daily habits and tasks. In the right column, rate each
task on a scale of 1 to 10 for how aligned it feels for you in your schedule. 1 is out
of alignment; 10 feels like something you would do no matter where you are.
This is an exercise to feel into the different levels or degrees of alignment. For
example, for me, I stretch, hydrate, connect to my breath, and have a cappuccino early each morning. This is 10/10 in alignment for me wherever I am in the
world and whomever is there with me.

Once you have rated each habit and task, review the list and notice how many tasks are or are closest to a 10. These ratings mean those tasks are in alignment and something you want to maintain in your daily schedule. If you have several things in your list that you rate under a 5, maybe those are habits that could fall away, leaving space for more meaningful practices to take root.

Once you've adjusted your list to your liking, see if implementing some changes to your routine helps or hinders your days.

GUIDED INTEGRATION

In the beginning of our work together, it is essential to take the practices and teaching seriously. However, try your best to not take your*self* so seriously. Between your devoted Mornings with Meaning, connecting to silence, meeting your inner guru, and learning about which feelings and emotions you want to embody in your life, you're on the path toward your most authentic, joyful life.

Know that you are allowed to desire more. I shared with you the beginning of my spiritual and self-development journey because I don't believe that I am unique. I've connected with so many of you who have also felt like you're the only one interested in spirituality, or that you want more out of your life. I also believe my story of experiencing anxiety was one of the greatest activators in bringing me to a spiritually aligned life. Perhaps this resonates with you, too.

Practice your Mornings with Meaning. Please show up for yourself and start implementing an eighteen-minute practice every day where you are connecting to your breath. Make it fun and accessible, but do it daily. It is essential to make time for yourself to have an embodied practice while reading this book.

Meet your inner guru. Your inner guru is your internal compass, a connection we need to deepen to show up for our most soul-authentic life. This relationship is rooted in admiration and trust within Self.

Get comfortable with the sound of silence. So many of us move through our lives filled with distraction, work, and sound. To tune inward, it can feel good to find moments of silence to connect with your inner guru. Try practicing silence in your home from 9:00 p.m. to 9:00 a.m. or opt for a getaway silent retreat.

Seek feeling-states, not goals. When on the self-development path, it is essential to ask yourself, *How do I want to feel?* This question can be answered with a specific feeling-state, like calm, or a metaphor, like a warm bath after a fun day in nature. This is going to look different for every single person, and it will guide you to experiencing your most nourishing life.

CHAPTER 2

facing
false gurus

*How would you behave if you knew you were a god or a goddess? How would
you treat yourself, how would you treat others? What kind of consciousness
would you hold about your smallest actions if you knew their effects influenced
the entire rest of creation? . . . If your awakenings could bring joy to the
multitudes? What kind of mindfulness would that inspire?*

—ANODEA JUDITH, EASTERN BODY, WESTERN MIND

"Sex is the best antidote for suffering," Guru Ashwin said, licking his already-moist lips. He stepped forward to embrace me. "Sexual relations will bring forth the intimacy you long for." After months of living in India and spending several days at his ashram in Rishikesh in Northern India, I'd been missing my family and friends, but I knew for sure that having sex with a false guru was not the cure for my loneliness. "Let us have sex together," he said, running a clammy hand along my bare shoulder. A wise voice within me said, *Run!* I ducked under his arm, dashed to my room, grabbed my backpack, and hightailed it out of that ashram.

What the actual fuck?

I kept replaying the situation over and over in my head. How did I end up here? I walked around Rishikesh, thinking about how it all felt like a movie. As the sun was setting, I reflected on what had led up to this moment in time. I'd landed in Mumbai months earlier to work with a nongovernmental organization (NGO) supporting hygiene efforts in the slum villages of Mumbai. I was aligned with the mission and wanted to support the project, and I knew that if I was going to have my parents' blessing to move to another continent, I needed a plan. This NGO allowed me to settle into Indian culture and meet like-minded people, and it offered me a sound footing so I could continue to explore India and live in yoga ashrams when the two-month commitment was complete.

I arrived in Mumbai around midnight one early fall night. At customs, I stood in line with a sweet English couple in their late sixties. They wore fedoras, were already dressed in Indian garb, and looked well-traveled and chic. We got to chitchatting. They had been to India many times and offered me a piece of advice that led my heart for many days: "Feast your eyes on all the colors, all the scents, all the energy of India." So, I did.

During my fellowship, I fell in love with Mumbai. My day-to-day life differed greatly from my American upbringing and was also different from the life I'd led in Israel just six months prior. I lived in a large Muslim village where my NGO housing was based, and worked in a slum village, an hour's train ride away. My fellowship introduced me to the local Jewish Indian community and I fostered wonderful friendships. During my fellowship, I googled local yogic teachers and discovered Dhana, a disciple of a great yogic master in an active meditation lineage. Some mornings, I'd wake up and prepare for my work in the slums while moving into a couple of sun salutations in my room. Other times, I walked through the village of Byculla before sunrise, in time for morning Sadhana—morning sacred practice—with Dhana. To get to Dhana's apartment, I'd shuffle in the dark past the slum dwellers, past people sleeping on the streets, and past roaming goats. Roosters crowed and the sweet smell of morning chai, a milk-based tea, followed me on my morning hike. I looked out of place, a fair-skinned female, alone, with vast slums in all directions. I wanted to keep a low profile, so I wrapped my hair in a scarf and moved like a shadow. The first time I arrived at Dhana's home, honestly, her jaw dropped. She was shocked to see a white girl at her doorpost at 6:30 a.m.

Dhana had a charming old two-bedroom apartment that had been passed down, generation to generation, from her grandmother. Sometimes Dhana's grandmother was there to greet me. Even though she was frail—a gust of wind could have blown her away—her eyes were filled with light. She greeted me by putting her hands on my face and looking into the depths of my eyes. Such a sweet soul. Dhana spoke perfect English; her grandmother and I spoke through smiles, laughs, and warm hugs. Dhana lovingly forced me to eat a Nagpur orange (as I always arrived flushed from my journey), and then we flowed through a breathwork sequence. Those early mornings at Dhana's taught me core Indian concepts of welcoming and hospitality and initiated my yogic wisdom into the power of active meditation, specifically algorithmic breathwork. I loved learning from Dhana and sitting with her in the early mornings.

My fellowship days were filled with gorgeous barefoot children running around smiling. However, the smell hits you before you even walk through the village—it's a mixture of curry spices and unstructured plumbing. Children squat out and about and have their morning bowel movements among discarded plastic bags and candy wrappers. Pigs run wild and free. Flies occupy every space. Homes are pinned together with steel materials and tarps, yet many shacks still have satellite dishes for television. Watching some Indian movies had partially prepared me for Mumbai and helped me overcome the initial shock of the slums, but nothing can ever prepare you for your first sight of children living in abject poverty. Still, what sticks with me today is the joy, the laughter, and the people's gusto for life.

The school days were filled with the smiling faces of young children wanting to learn. Many of the children had access to American TV, so there were a few English phrases we could use to communicate. We educated the kids on handwashing, introduced them to soap and how to use it, sang songs about brushing teeth, and taught them some basic English and Hindi phrases. The residents of this part of Mumbai speak a local language called Marathi, and one of the agendas of supporting children in the slums is to offer them a beginner's level understanding of Hindi, India's national language. If these children learn Hindi, they can access more opportunity around India, so I learned some basic Hindi phrases. We also had Hindi speaking guides with us at all times, which was necessary for language barriers and navigating the slums.

After teaching in the morning, I'd head to my favorite yoga studio in the Bollywood area, then meet friends for dinner, and then return to my tiny apartment to map out travel plans for once my fellowship was over.

For the ten-day-long Diwali holiday, I got some time off from educating in the slums. Diwali is the Festival of Lights, a Hindu religious festival celebrated all over India. It is comparable to what Westerners would consider the Christmas/New Year's break. I had been living in Mumbai for a month and a half, and I wanted to explore different parts of the country. I'd always been fascinated by Ayurveda. After extensive googling, I booked a stay at an Ayurvedic ashram in Rishikesh, Northern India. This area was well known because the Beatles once spent about three months there, at the ashram of their guru, Maharishi Mahesh Yogi, who was famous in the Transcendental Meditation lineage.

Ayurveda is a Sanskrit word that translates as "pathways of life." Ayurveda offers a road map to healthy living, disease prevention, and longevity as defined by three doshas, or categories, known as Pitta, Vata, and Kapha. The doshas are routes to understanding yourself, your digestive system, and what foods may be best for your body type. Yoga and meditation are stems of Ayurveda, and the asanas (yoga postures) can be targeted based on which dosha matches a person's physical characteristics. I am fascinated by how much the Indian and Nepalese cultures use Ayurvedic techniques to heal and inform a healthy lifestyle even today.

Rishikesh hosts a small airport, and when I stepped off the plane I felt immediate relief to be closer to nature (there's constant hustle and movement in Mumbai). There was more space to breathe in Rishikesh. Upon arriving at the Ayurvedic ashram, I felt the power of the Ganges River and appreciated all the colorful paper chains and floating mandala decorations for Diwali. The ashram sat on top of a hill, not far from the popular Ram Jhula Bridge. Flowers in orange and pink were spread across the lawn. It was beautiful.

The car I'd hired at the airport pulled up to the ashram and dropped me at the front gate. I walked inside. Not sure where to go, I sat on a bench at a table in the courtyard. The place seemed deserted. "Hello?" I said into the air, hoping someone would arrive.

Sure enough, a portly Indian man walked toward me and then brought his hands into namaskar, the prayer position at the heart. "Welcome," he said, with a slight bow of his head. He introduced himself as Ashwin, a yogi master, Ayurvedic doctor, and guru of the ashram. A bit of anxiety filled my chest in his presence. He walked me inside a nearby building and pulled out an intake form for me to fill out. An older man with a thick mustache arrived and offered me a tart-tasting juice to drink while I filled out the detailed form. His name tag read "Navi." Guru Ashwin, breathing heavily, surveyed me as I sat and asked me follow-up questions based on my written responses.

One of my spiritual practices is that I am always safe in my truth, so when the form asked about my reason for being here, I told Guru Ashwin that I was on a quest to experience spirituality in the East, immerse myself in yogic spiritual practices, and heal some anxiety and fear-based, or limiting, thought patterns. He asked if I had an awareness of physical pain in my body, and I told him I was experiencing tight hips. He raised his eyebrows. *Why is he raising his eyebrows?*

Then, he asked about my time living in Mumbai. "I've been feeling lonely," I said. "I miss the physical contact of my family and friends. At home, we hug and connect. . . . I'm not so keen on hugging strangers, ya know?" I ended with an awkward laugh. He didn't laugh. As I was deep into my spiritual journey, I wanted to receive insights from someone I believed to be more knowledgeable than me on topics I was interested in. So, of course, I was truthful about my current obstacles and felt human experience.

"Interesting," he said, and his gaze lingered on my face. "I recently got married to a match made by my parents," he said. It was a bit off topic but still intriguing. I had learned from my friends in Mumbai that matchmaking is a custom in Indian culture. Without me asking, Guru Ashwin shared more. "She and I have only met a few times, and I haven't heard from her in a while." His energy shifted. He seemed withdrawn, even sad. I thought he was about to cry. I was going to ask follow-up questions, more to be polite than being curious. But I was eager to check in, get to my room, freshen up, and rest from my journey. So, I nodded. His eyes lingered on my chest. I was wearing black leggings and a loose blue *kurti*, an Indian tunic that covered my body down to my knees and exposed only my bare elbows. I cleared my throat to refocus the conversation.

Guru Ashwin jotted down some notes, told me about the schedule of Ayurvedic ashram life, and showed me to my room. Navi carried my backpack. I smiled at him in gratitude, and as we had a language barrier, I used my basic Hindi skills to say thanks, *Shukriya*. The ashram room was stunning, overlooking the Himalayan Mountains, and had a view of the front garden. Navi placed my backpack on the floor while I opened the door to the bathroom. All I saw was a bucket. "Where's the shower?" I asked.

"We use buckets here," Ashwin said. He filled up an aged gray bucket with room-temperature water from the faucet. He used a nearby cup with a small spout, filled it from the bucket of water, and gestured, as if he was going to pour it down his body. He made an uncomfortable joke about helping me with my bucket bath should I need any assistance. I laughed to be polite, assuming there was a language barrier at play.

I thanked Guru Ashwin for his time and watched as he and Navi walked out. Guru Ashwin lingered by the door, surveying me. I walked over, guided him out, and locked the door. Even though the ashram was nice, the bed looked comfy, and the bucket bath sounded fun, something felt stale . . . a little off. There was only one other guest staying there, Margie, a woman from California who was celebrating her sixtieth birthday. I chalked my sketchy feelings up to my being so far outside of my comfort zone, and I let that feeling-state slip away as I prepared for bedtime.

Rishikesh is stunning. The following morning, I spent my first full day walking around the town, eating the most divine North Indian and Nepalese food, connecting with other expats, and taking two yoga classes—one with the morning sunrise, for morning Sadhana, and one before dinner as a midday/evening practice. Rishikesh has many Israeli travelers, which nourished my soul, as I'd spent the first half of the year living in Israel and was still working on my Hebrew. Seeing all the Israeli trekkers helped me feel like I wasn't so far away from home.

Returning to the Ayurvedic ashram, I ate a simple meal of chapati with ghee and slow-cooked chickpeas with a side of a local veggies. It was delicious! The chef offered me some sliced fruit for dessert, a melon to cool the body to prepare for sleep. Upon returning to my room, I rubbed some coconut oil in my hair and journaled before bed. My body felt calm, and I was eager to wake up for my morning Sadhana.

I awoke before sunrise. A crisp breeze off the river freshened my room. After oil pulling (an Ayurvedic practice of swishing high-quality coconut oil in your mouth to pull out bacteria), tongue scraping (using a copper scraper to remove excess yeast and the white coating on top of the tongue), and then drinking a warm tea, I joined Margie and together we moved into a morning asana flow. The standard Hatha yoga sequence felt nourishing, and I enjoyed gentle massage treatments with a female Ayurvedic practitioner. After the healing session, I decided to journal out in the ashram gardens.

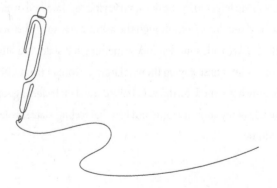

That afternoon, a young girl with long brown hair, about eleven years old, was walking around the ashram, spotted me, and beelined toward me. She pulled on my sleeve and held out her hand to show me the *mehndi*—henna plant dye used to make temporary tattoos—she had in her palm. I rolled up my sleeve in response, and she sat next to me and gave me a big smile, showing her beautiful, straight white teeth. I tried to communicate with her and through some hand gestures learned that she was Navi's daughter, Salma. The language barrier was deep, so we sat in silence for twenty minutes as she created a gorgeous mandala design up and down my left arm and hand. I relaxed, feeling the cool mehndi on my skin. Impressed by her flawless circular and symmetrical designs, I thanked her profusely. I wondered if it was appropriate to give her money or tip her, as our interaction had felt random, abrupt, and she was just a child. Salma left me to journal, and I lay in the sun, allowing the design to dry before heading to my room to recharge.

About twenty minutes after I'd returned to my room, there was a knock at the door. Curious, I opened it slowly. Salma stood there with a note in her hand. She placed the worn-through piece of paper in my palm, walked into my room, plopped onto my bed, and made herself at home. Confused, I looked at the note and saw that it was beautifully handwritten in English. I was certain Salma didn't know a lick of English. Still standing at the door, I read the note, which explained that Salma needed dental work imperative for her health, but her parents couldn't afford the procedure. The note ended by asking if I (or the person reading it) would give Salma five thousand Indian rupees to pay for her dental work.

Oh, I realized after a beat. *She was asking for money.* I walked over to her, smiled, took her hands in mine, and gave them a gentle squeeze.

My first instinct was how grateful I felt that I could help Salma get the care she needed. I was flattered that she'd felt safe enough after our brief interaction

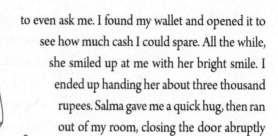

to even ask me. I found my wallet and opened it to see how much cash I could spare. All the while, she smiled up at me with her bright smile. I ended up handing her about three thousand rupees. Salma gave me a quick hug, then ran out of my room, closing the door abruptly behind her.

Instead of feeling happy that I could help her, I ended up feeling a bit flustered. *That was weird.* So, I walked over to Margie's room to get her perspective on the situation.

Margie was waking up from an afternoon nap. I told her what had just happened with Navi's daughter. "Oh, honey." Margie looked at me with pity. "You just got scammed." We looked at each other. We chuckled, then laughed, then delighted in some full, roaring belly laughs. It was an outrageous moment. Things like this happen sometimes—life is random and keeps you on your toes. We cannot always control what happens, but once we learn the full picture, we can edit how we react. I realized that I'd known it before Margie said it—I'd been totally scammed. I was mostly at peace, however. I felt like I'd paid Salma for my mehndi tattoo, a fair trade-off. Even so, I would have preferred to just pay for the service. Still laughing, Margie and I walked together to dinner in the ashram's garden.

Guru Ashwin found me during mealtime as the evening was about to end. He broke into my conversation with Margie by talking again about how he was married but hadn't heard from his "wife" since the day their matchmaking contract was set. Uncomfortable, I changed the topic and asked him to share some of his spiritual practices with us. Guru Ashwin shared that he wakes up at 3:00 a.m. and goes for a walk, sometimes with his father. Then he prays, meditates, and moves into a gentle asana sequence. He goes back to sleep until after sunrise, then wakes up to begin the workday. Wanting to learn more, I asked him follow-up questions. I was fascinated by what he was telling me, but he kept scooching closer to me (and I kept shifting away), paying me extra-special attention, and basically ignoring Margie. It was uncomfortable and unnerving.

"I've thought a lot about what you said," Guru Ashwin said quietly, licking his lips as he placed a hand on my thigh. I stood up to leave. "In the spirit of assisting you on your spiritual journey, I am happy to help, and since I haven't heard from my wife ..." He stepped forward to hug me. "Sex is the best antidote for suffering," he whispered. His voice trailed off as he ran his other hand along my bare shoulder. "Let us have sex together."

Run.

After a swift goodbye to Margie, I ducked under Guru Ashwin's arm, rushed to my room, and grabbed my stuff. I replayed his vile, false-guru behavior as I ran out of the ashram. I had no plan, nowhere to sleep, and the sun was setting. It was December, and the temperature was dropping. But I knew I had to leave, that I wouldn't feel comfortable or safe if I stayed. I knew that as long as I listened to my inner guru, I would be okay. Still, here I was, all alone in Rishikesh. Night was falling. I was feeling lost and, I admit, anxious.

Help. I need help. As I walked around, I practiced a gentle walking meditation to relax my nervous system, calm my mind, and control my breath: a simple inhale for four steps, hold for four steps, exhale for four steps, and hold the exhale. I had everything I owned on my back and just enough rupees left in my wallet to find a place to sleep. But what I wanted more than anything was to feel safe, which to me meant meeting warm, welcoming people. Then I could sleep tonight and continue my journey. But I didn't know anyone in Rishikesh!

As I walked down the Ram Jhula, I prayed. Monkeys dangling from the wires of the bridge witnessed my rising panic attack. My inner guru got me out of that ashram, and now I needed a higher power to guide me to the next safe place. *Dear God and the God of my ancestors, please guide me at this moment. I feel so scared. I need to feel safe. Please guide me to kind people. Please make it obvious. Send me a sign to let me know I am going to be okay.* Tears ran down my face and my stomach grumbled. *I can't believe I'm hungry at a time like this!*

As I was walking down the road, I tried to hold my head high. I breathed. Two roads diverged, and I chose the path that had fewer people on it but was more well-lit. It felt more welcoming. I saw a large yellow sign hanging from an old lamppost. Underneath it stood two people, fellow backpackers. They were glowing—legitimately glowing—and staring straight at me. We made the type of eye contact you see in movies. We were drawn to each other. I walked over and these two sweet people, Penny and Eli (who, it turned out, had met each other only hours earlier), shook my hand. "Hi," they said. We decided to find a café together.

Penny hailed from outside Amsterdam and Eli was a New Yorker with a thick accent who was living in Tulum, Mexico. We played our Jewish geography (a cultural game that usually starts with, "Do you know this person?") and discovered we had distant connections, a confirmation to me from the universe that I was safe. My heart relaxed. I explained to them what had just happened, and Penny gave me an enormous hug, filled with older-sister energy. She had just finished her yoga teacher training in Dharamshala, a more northern city, and as we walked around Rishikesh, she told me about her course curriculum.

I went with them to an out-of-the-way Nepalese restaurant for fresh juice and curry. I felt such extreme relief to be in the presence of these fellow yogis.

"Erin, that guy is staring at you," said my new soul friend, Eli. And sure enough, as I turned around to look, he was right. A bearded man about my age was looking at me across the café. I was coming down from a heightened emotional state, so it took me a beat to ground my breath.

After a moment, I recognized him. When I'd been living in Jerusalem a few months earlier, he'd often made green juice for me at a local juice bar in the Machane Yehuda market. I walked over, said, "מה נשמע?" or "What's up?" in Hebrew, and felt immense gratitude for seeing a familiar face. My anxiety vanished. I felt warm, safe, welcomed—and supported by my inner guru that I'd made the right decision by leaving the sketchy ashram. After reconnecting with my friend and exchanging phone numbers, Penny and I ended up rooming together at another yoga ashram for the next week. It was about six dollars a day for two meals, two yoga classes, and sleeping accommodations.

I've discovered that when you trust in your inner voice, miracles happen. In my case, leaving the ashram was a no-brainer. But I had no idea what would happen next—and being alone in an unfamiliar place is unnerving. Each time we are put in a challenging situation where the only person who can save us is ourselves, we increase our connection to ourself and our inner guru. Maybe you can think of a time when you too were alone, fearful, and needed to dig deep and pull through.

I've found myself in some shocking situations I never could have prepared myself for or anticipated. Often, when we are on a self-development journey, we trust that someone else has the answers or will know what is best for us. To balance your natural curiosity and love of learning, you need to base your decisions on what feels clear, comfortable, and safe for *you*.

Note: *If you are processing severe trauma, please seek out professional help from a mental health professional. If you have been manipulated or scammed and* *made a choice that you regretted later on, please be gentle with yourself. You were doing the best you could, given the tools you had at that moment. Getting taken advantage of can happen sometimes when we are curious and go outside our zone of comfort. There is a layer of goodness involved in trusting someone, and when you connect with your inner guru, that guide will let you know if the person you're leaning toward trusting is, in fact, acting with integrity.*

WALKING MEDITATION: BOX BREATHING

This controlled breathwork meditation is a wonderful practice to slow down your nervous system and connect to your breath while on the move. It is a beginner's level meditation and a practice you can weave into a full life schedule or when you're in the thick of a panic and need a movement practice to return to calm.

While on a walk or commuting from point A to point B, implement box breathing. If you have a stuffy nose, you may want to blow your nose before the practice to increase nasal air flow.

To start, empty all the air from your lungs. Inhale through your nose for a count of four steps, hold for four steps, and exhale through your nose for a count of four steps. Hold the exhale for four steps. Continue this breathing pattern for three to five minutes.

This gentle practice, often referred to as square breathing, became well known as a breathwork tool to support Navy Seals to stay calm and increase focus. I love this equal breathing pattern, as the deep breathwork leads to relaxation and inner ease. Integrate this practice on your next walk.

YOGIC BREATH MEDITATION

When you are in a stressful or emotionally activated situation, you will default to your fight, flight, or freeze primal response, or you will default to your most common habits. Here's a breathing exercise that can help you move through an energetically charged event.

Take a moment to ground yourself in a safe space, then start your yogic breath.

This is a two-part inhale and one part exhale.

Inhale through your nose; your lower belly expands. Inhale through your nose; your upper chest expands. Exhale through your mouth and make a sound. A gentle sigh, "Ahh…" may feel good.

Repeat this practice for three to five minutes or until you feel your body relaxing. Once your body is in a relaxed state, ask yourself, "What must occur for me to sleep tonight?" Stay in this energy until you have a clear next step on what you need to do.

The yogic breath is essential, as it provides abundant oxygen to the brain; slows down the fight, flight, or freeze response; and relaxes the nervous system. When the nervous system is regulated, clarity around decision-making is possible.

Framing the question, "What must occur for me to sleep tonight?" is important because when you're asleep, you're the most vulnerable. For sleep to come, regardless of your exhaustion level, you need to feel that you're safe. When you want to align with a decision, work with that question.

RELEASE PRACTICE

Try this practice when you are spiraling, overwhelmed, stressed, or in a negative thought pattern. This is an effective way to release a powerful emotion (like a cry or a scream), but it takes time—at least twenty minutes, and up to an hour, if you can. As you dive into this practice, it is important that you feel safe.

Lie down on your back with your phone near you. Try listening to a playlist you love. Choose music with deep drums and sensual voices. Take up space. Be comfy. You can lie in your bed, on the floor on a yoga mat, or even on a grassy area in a private space outside. Place the soles of your feet together and let your knees spread wide, in *supta baddha konasana*. This looks like making a diamond shape with your legs.

Inhale through your nose for a slow count of five. Hold at the top for a beat and make loud, audible exhales through your mouth for a slow count of eight. Maintain this breathing pattern for ten minutes. These exhales are a deep release, and each one is important as you loosen and release tension from your body through your breath.

Turn up the music. Keep focusing on your long, audible exhales for ten more minutes. Moan and sigh. Release. Be here. You may feel vulnerable and emotional, and that's okay. Do this for a minimum of twenty minutes.

After the session, check in with yourself. If you like, you can journal after this session. Maybe you cried and released. Maybe you feel lighter. Maybe you need a nap. All feelings are welcome.

Trust your body.
It knows what it needs.

RITUAL: HOME IS WHERE YOU ARE

Whenever I travel, I have specific protocols to make sure
I feel comfy, cozy, and safe in a temporary space.
Here are some of my favorite practices to imple-
ment in new sleeping spaces.

First, settle in. Maybe you brought a white
noise machine, ear plugs, and a book with
you. Place your personal objects nearby—picture frames, reading glasses, evening moisturizer,
an eye mask. These niche items symbolize that you
are home.

Open a window and allow in fresh air. This is vital if you're staying in a stuffy
room, as the fresh air can shift the energy in a space. This symbolizes out with
the old and in with the you.

Create an altar. Early on in my travels, I would create a proper altar every-
where I traveled. This would be a corner of the space I was staying in, with my
mala beads, essential oils, manifestations written on paper, and sacred mantra
deck or oracle cards. I would use a shawl as a tablecloth and lay crystals around
it. If you don't want a formal altar, you could also try placing personal items
near your bed.

As I move into sleep on my first night in a new space, I practice gratitude.
Here is a simple prayer I use: "Thank you for allowing me to arrive here safely.
Please bless this space and protect me while I reside here. May I honor this space
as it honors me."

GUIDED INTEGRATION

In this chapter, I brought you to my life in India, picturing the slums and learning about some parts of Indian culture. I shared a pivotal story on my spiritual journey that activated the fight-or-flight response while also strengthening my relationship to my inner guru. In those moments what matters is our own well-being, and that we have the agency to stand up for ourselves and get out of the situation if necessary. We learned some tools for dealing with acute stress in the moment, as well as how to recover and recharge once we're safely out of harm's way.

- ☀ **Ask yourself, *What is the next best step?*** If you want to move to a new city but don't know anyone who lives there, maybe secure an internship, a job offer, or a grad school acceptance letter, and build as many connections off of that introduction as you can.

- ☀ **You are always safe in your truth.** You are never wrong when you are speaking from your heart. Just make sure that whoever you're sharing your heart with is in integrity.

- ☀ **Practice yogic breathing techniques.** You can't always think your way out of a problem—or there simply isn't time to. Knowing yogic breathing can help calm your nervous system and put you in a better headspace to assess and decide when you're ready.

- ☀ **Allow the breath to release.** This is one of my most favorite practices of allowing stale air to leave the body through deep, long, and audible exhales. Try this when you are feeling stressed or anxious and need to release some emotional burdens.

※ **Create ritual wherever you are.** Whether you are a full-time nomad or on a short trip, take time to create a sacred altar in your room. This allows you to practice gratitude for arriving safely in a new space, feel grounded, and mark this spot as your temporary home.

※ **Seek out help when you need it.** Whether that's leaning on a family member or close friend, or working with a mental health professional or trusted spiritual guide, you don't need to face difficult situations alone. Beware of false gurus—and be open to receiving help from people you feel safe with and trust.

in the face
of a trigger,
express the truth

Integrity is choosing courage over comfort;
it's choosing what's right over what's fun, fast, or easy;
and it's practicing your values, not just professing them.

—BRENÉ BROWN, *DARE TO LEAD*

Om Gam Ganapataye Namaha. The yoga teacher at my mostly silent ashram in Kerala, South India, continued the morning chanting prayer. The students' powerful chants blended into the background. Outside, the sky was dark as the sun had yet to rise . . . and I? I was thinking about how sweaty my bangs will look, stuck to my forehead after a full day of asana. Should I grow out my bangs? Should I trim my bangs? Or let them be? Should I use the nail clippers in my Dopp kit and create a "fringe" look?

This yoga teacher training was not a good fit for me, but I wanted to receive the prestigious 200-hour yoga teacher certification while still in India. So, I stayed and used the time to learn all the diverse methods for dropping into meditation. I snuck a look at my fellow yogis all around me. Some of them held their posture erect, repeated the chant, and kept their eyes closed. Others were staring up at the sky, awaiting the orange sunrise. This yoga school was beautiful, overlooking the greenery of Kerala, but it was small, and we could leave only one day a week, on Fridays. I was experiencing extreme cabin fever, stuck in this tight Buddha-bootcamp space. I found it suffocating that we couldn't leave— my body was craving a walk that was over thirty steps. *Om Gam Ganapataye Namaha.* . . . I closed my eyes, came back to the chant, and anchored myself in my breath. I noticed the sensation of air flowing in and out of my nostrils and allowed it to bring me back to my meditation.

I shifted my posture and rolled up a mat to place beneath my tailbone, rotating my pelvis forward and relaxing the pelvic floor. This is a gentle hip opener and felt intuitive in my body. I relaxed my shoulders down and rotated them back just a touch while straightening my posture. I've noticed that the more relaxed my body is, the deeper I can drop into a meditation. The biggest shift for me is moving my heart toward the heavens. This subtle heart opener—power pose even—keeps my chest lifted and makes me feel happy, light, and positive. *Om Gam Ganapataye Namaha*. . . . I inhaled and exhaled between mantras, coming back to the air flowing in and out of my nostrils.

Silent seated practice before our asana yoga class was the most difficult for me. This is when you sit down on your mat or bolster and drop into meditation right away. This is challenging and may not resonate . . . and it doesn't always work. (I've since learned that it doesn't work for many of my clients, either.) During the month-long training, I sometimes woke up extra early for self-practice, to open my shoulders and hips to prepare for the morning meditation. The movement was necessary to get my energy flowing and to prepare my mind and body for silent seated meditation that led into a day filled with asanas.

Besides most meals and some class time in silence, we also practiced silence all day on Thursdays and could leave the ashram and explore Kerala on Fridays. Silence was encouraged from lights out to breakfast.

My principal teacher and the owner of the ashram was an older Indian man, Sudhir, with a son about my age. He called me "little girl," as I was the youngest in the group. Sudhir praised the most flexible students and pushed our backs to make us stretch deeper. One time he pressed on my back so hard I heard my hamstring groan. One day, in philosophy class, Sudhir shared that he believes children with special needs are birthed to parents with bad karma. "Bad people in past lives receive kids with retardation," were his exact words. I remember my yogic classmates nodding in agreement. No one reacted, except for my one friend Laura, who rolled her eyes. I almost screamed. It was a sick, outrageous comment. "That's insane," I blurted out. "It's inappropriate. Some of the best, most loving people I have ever met are neurodivergent." No one else chimed in. I knew his words were false, but it concerned me to my core that no one else seemed disturbed by Sudhir's teachings.

Sudhir wouldn't answer any of my questions, shushed and silenced me, and kept making us switch bedrooms, leaving me feeling very ungrounded. I didn't like him and thought his beliefs and teachings were toxic. But the thing that scared me the most was that no one questioned him! Sudhir calls himself a yogi master. He can lay his upper body flat onto his legs and show off his flexibility, but no one questioned the dangerous comments he often made in passing. It was a hard lesson for me—some people are suggestible. They don't take time to get curious, question authority, or think for themselves.

One day, over a community meal of dal and chapati, one participant, Marty, and I were seated next to one another. We were talking about our spiritual paths. I mentioned my earlier job leading trips to Poland and living in Israel and how it was one of the most important parts of my life. "It realigned me to the path I am on right now," I told him. I shared that I'd educated youth about the Holocaust and World War II.

Marty interrupted me. "The Holocaust didn't happen," he said. He didn't even look up from his plate.

His words hit me as I took a bite of dal. I choked. My eyes watered, and my instinct was to fight, flee, and cry all at the same time. "What?" I am fighting for my sanity to survive this intense ashram experience, and now I have to deal with a Holocaust denier?

"I have stood in Auschwitz, Birkenau, and Majdanek," I said. "I have been there four times. I have held the hands of survivors and even have some friends with grandparents who survived the Holocaust. There is endless evidence that it occurred." My heart rate increased, my voice was shaking with passion, and even though I was certain with my words, I felt repulsion.

Everyone else at the table heard the conversation and no one even reacted. Of course, we weren't supposed to react. We were students of yoga committed to peace and calm. The first "rule" on the spiritual path is understanding that the only thing we can control is our reactions. But a Holocaust-denier yogi? I'd taken one hundred-plus students from Auschwitz to Birkenau and into the death camp of Majdanek. I was so close to gaslighting myself spiritually and staying calm—after all, I was devoted to the yogic path, wasn't I? But my inner guru told me it didn't matter how much I was meditating, or how deep I was on the spiritual path. Was I being genuine to allow a Holocaust denier to say something so sickening? To allow his vile words to just hang there in that room? No. My inner alignment begged me to speak up.

"You're misinformed," I said. I shared statistics about the six million Jews who died in the Holocaust. "Do you want to see the photos I took when I visited the camps?" I listened to his patronizing responses, then told him he sounded like a false yogi, like the one I'd met in Rishikesh. He grumbled under his breath and got up to clean his plate before leaving the room. I wasn't committed to being right. That wasn't the point. I was listening to my inner guru, being real, and speaking authentically. Because when we are sitting in silence, I find myself continuously coming back to this thought: It is more important for me to live and speak in integrity than to be a well-behaved yogi.

Even though this situation was intense and out of alignment, I trusted myself. I knew this was not the route for me. This was not the guide for me, and the other participants in the training didn't need to be my lifelong spiritual soul friends. *And that was okay.* This took the pressure off. I stayed because I wanted to show myself that I could stay calm, grounded, and connected to my inner guru even in these uncomfortable and, frankly, provoking circumstances.

I've heard new mothers say, "The days are long, but the years are short." That saying came to mind when the ashram days trickled by. I could feel the clock standing still. But then a week would pass. We'd have a day off and I'd think, *Huh, that was fast!* Time will always keep moving. It is the one consistent thing about our human experience. I made friends with time. I learned I could do anything for a month, and that I could (and would) take this time to find the practices that resonated with me.

During this time of self-reflection I found unique techniques that supported my own personal meditation journey, one being the most potent—gratitude. I sat in meditation, focused on relaxed, gentle breathing, and thought about how excited I would be to see my sister, Danielle, when I returned home from India—how cute she is when she smiles, the blue of her eyes, and how she sleeps with her wand from Harry Potter World. I thought about how proud I was of my brother, Matthew, for chasing his dreams to become a baseball scout; how much I appreciated the support my mother gave me in all situations, her city girl attitude, and her Chicago pride; and how much I loved hearing my dad's laugh, his entrepreneurial spirit, and how he always made Mom feel like the most special lady in the room.

I cried.
I released.
I relaxed.

Gratitude changed everything for me. From there, I drifted off into a deep meditation, the mantra blurred in the background. The meditation was so deep, I could feel my cells releasing and filling with white light. It was the type of meditation you have that when you come back into the physical world, you feel like you just slept for eight hours. This gratitude practice became my route to the sacred, anchoring me and offering a needed tool to guide me into a powerful, silent, seated meditation.

If you've ever elected to tough out a situation, what was it that made you want to stay? Do you think those were good reasons? For me, completing a 200-hour yoga teacher training certificate was a goal I wasn't willing to give up on because of a couple bigoted participants. I learned to tolerate the discomfort and found solace in reminding myself that just because I was in a situation I didn't enjoy didn't mean I needed to compromise my integrity to fit in. I owed it to myself and to others to speak the truth. I also learned what a powerful tool gratitude can be. Yes, it lifts our spirits in a day-to-day kind of way. But it's also important to foster an attitude of gratitude when facing a challenging situation—conflicts at work, a scary diagnosis from the doctor, a fraught relationship with a family member. Gratitude lends us strength when we feel overwhelmed by life's challenges.

Self-discovery can be hard work—we're dredging up the past, coming to terms with feelings and facts we might've neglected in the present, and bracing for big changes in the future. It's a huge challenge figuring out who we really are and what we really want, but we're also going to need to consider how we'll stay true to ourselves in the real world. What happens when others challenge us and our beliefs? Do we stay true to ourselves at any cost? Do we keep the peace, or do we make waves? These are important themes when it comes to maintaining integrity.

MAINTAINING YOUR INTEGRITY

While on my spiritual journey, I felt pressured to live up to some themes that were deemed "spiritual." In the name of purity, I was vegan for a long time even though my body craved meat. In the name of peace, I didn't stand up for myself in times of conflict because I didn't want to disturb the moment. But choosing peace led me to feel worse, because I felt I'd let myself and my inner guru down.

Don't limit your self-expression because you believe identifying as one thing means you need to silence another part of yourself. There is room to be many things at once. As Walt Whitman famously said,

"I am large, I contain multitudes."

On my journey of living in India, I felt like I'd allowed parts of myself to die because a thought or opinion I'd had was deemed outside the context of "love and light." Love and light, my ass. I've seen many wonderful people on the spiritual path edit their true selves in the name of fitting into a spiritual box. So, let's call it what it is: spiritual bypassing. This happens when we use spiritual methods to avoid dealing with unresolved emotional or psychological obstacles or issues. It is when we convince ourselves to "stay positive" even though we are hurting inside and need some time to feel the wound and process the emotions. But focusing on positivity or subduing your personality rather than having those hard conversations doesn't serve you. Having hard conversations and standing up for what you believe in—or are a trained expert in—is important as we walk this spiritual path.

ACCOUNTING OF THE SOUL

I have learned that embodying genuine work in the spiritual world means committing to your most authentic Self. Accounting of the Soul is a sacred Hebrew practice of taking time to check in with yourself, learn more about yourself, and implement self-study. Once you know who you are, at your core, you know how to move through the day—you know what is meant for you. This inner check-in provides the tools you need to live your most soul-authentic life, because you know what your intention is, and you know if you need course correction.

Accounting of the Soul aligns with our Mornings with Meaning practice, as when we account for the soul, we embody the intention that lights us up. These two practices go hand in hand. They both honor reflection, whereby we take a moment, slow down, and check in.

JOURNAL PROMPTS

Practicing Accounting of the Soul

How am I, truly? Am I showing up in a way that would make my younger Self proud? Was I the best version of myself yesterday? What is my intention for today? What are five things I can do today to embody that intention?

AN ATTITUDE OF GRATITUDE

A 2009 study by the National Institutes of Health (NIH) suggests that when we practice gratitude, life satisfaction can improve. NIH researchers measured blood flow in participants' brains while they thought about what they were grateful for and observed more activity in the hypothalamus—the area that governs eating, temperature, sex drive, sleeping, heart rate, and thirst. This study suggests that when we practice gratitude, by thinking of all the people and things for which we are grateful, we improve our sleep, become motivated to engage in physical activity, and even lower daily stress.

Gratitude changed everything for me. It allowed me to drift off into deep meditation. My gratitude practice became my route to the sacred, and I believe it can have powerful benefits for you too, should you find yourself in a challenging situation that you need or want to make the best of.

ACTIVE GRATITUDE MEDITATION

If you want to shift your energy and realign with the present moment, try this meditation practice. It will also feel good if you're experiencing anxiety and want to return to a calm, centered, relaxed state.

To start, sit in a comfortable posture or lie down—whatever feels best in your body. Then think of one thing you are grateful for in your life. Inhale and connect your thumb and pinkie finger. As you exhale, say out loud what you are grateful for.

Repeat this with your next finger: Inhale, connect your thumb and ring finger, and recite another thing you are grateful for as you exhale. Continue this pattern with each finger, inhaling, connecting your thumb and finger, and saying aloud something you are grateful for as you exhale. Repeat until you reach eight gratitudes. Continue the practice if it feels good.

The intent of this practice is to "trip" into gratitude, and to be present with all the wonderful things that have happened and are happening in your life. It's okay if the present moment doesn't reflect how you want to feel in the future. Coming into a state of gratitude will support your alignment and redirection. Start partaking in a gratitude practice today and notice your mood shift over time.

GUIDED INTEGRATION

In this chapter, we looked at what happens when others challenge our boundaries and our values, and how to cope with conflict. It is powerful to recognize that something is out of alignment and yet elect to explore the situation to learn from it. This is also a time to navigate who the true Self is and what standing up for your beliefs means to you.

- ☀ **Spirituality is not a one-size-fits-all model.** If you are interested in many diverse theologies, you can get sucked into the beliefs and practices of an educator who may not be the best guide for you. As with any curiosity, take what resonates, leave what doesn't.

- ☀ **Maintain your integrity.** There is a lot of pressure to cave, to fit in, to just conform and be like all those around you. However, trusting your truth is one way you communicate with your inner guru and anchor in on your own personal integrity. Stand up for what you believe in. Check in with yourself often; practice your Accounting of the Soul.

❊ **Make gratitude a daily practice.** Maybe you can find something valuable in going through a tough situation. Or maybe there are other things you are grateful for that can prop you up when you are feeling low and in need of strength. Do not underestimate the value of taking time and reciting gratitudes to bring you back into a healthy headspace.

CHAPTER 4

discovering your personal strengths

Instead of understanding depression as a chemical imbalance we have to overcome, or a mood disorder we have to be in charge of, what if it were just the result of us not being able to use our strengths? What if it were just us feeling blocked from being who we truly are?

—DAN TOMASULO, LEARNED HOPEFULNESS

"I lost control the other day," a woman shared with our overeater's group. "I was at a family gathering, feeling very stressed out by work, and even though I ate normally in the company of my family, afterward I went home and binged." Her honesty struck a chord. Her words were real, and I felt them land on my heart. It was refreshing to hear someone speak from their soul. I lit up because I saw myself in her.

Calling in to the overeater's group was not routine for me. I had called in that night because I was feeling understimulated, disconnected from my spiritual path. The daily conversations I was having lacked depth. I was using food as a tool to "fill myself up," and to cope with the wintertime blues. At this point, I was a (mostly) healthful and balanced eater, but there were moments when I was still seeking enjoyment in an extra helping, well past the point of feeling full. So, I called. I related deeply to some of the pain points shared on the call. Food doesn't talk back. It can be entertaining and soothing to occupy the mouth. But at my core, even though I was eating three-plus square meals a day, I was starved spiritually.

There have been many moments in which I have felt the light in me was blown out. This feeling sat in my heart, painted dark purple. It felt similar to stale energy, like the stiffness in your legs when you've been sitting all day. This feeling, which was always more prominent during Chicago winters, became even stronger during my spiritual journey. In the West, we call this depression, or maybe seasonal affective disorder (SAD). But those diagnoses never resonated with me—I believed I was happy and had a healthy relationship with myself and my loved ones. I just felt kind of blah, a feeling I learned later was my cue that I was understimulated. Maybe you've experienced this feeling-state as well.

At Columbia, I took a life-changing positive psychology course with Dr. Dan Tomasulo. Of all the brilliant topics I studied, I found learning about personal strengths to be transformational when it came to healing understimulation and living a nourishing life. Identifying personal strengths is my go-to exercise for clients who are feeling seasonal depression, depression, burnout, disconnection from Self, or understimulation. I also refer to this framework when I learn from my clients that they are trying to "fill themselves up" with an unhealthful pattern such as excessive alcohol or drug use, extreme promiscuity, compulsive shopping, or, like for myself, overeating.

Positive psychology translates into what makes life worth living. Over time, scientists have learned that positive emotions and positive thoughts are nutrients for the soul and lead to a happier life. Those who study positive psychology have happiness down to a science. We are all unique, as no one has experienced life quite the way you have. However, there are specific formulas and protocols that can help you increase your level of happiness. One particularly powerful tool is the PERMA model, developed by Dr. Martin Seligman at the University of Pennsylvania.

The PERMA Model

In his 2011 book *Flourish*, Seligman puts language to the tools and actions to increase well-being and happiness. The PERMA model introduces five principal components that lead to a life of increased joy, nourishment, and connection:

- ❀ P = Positive emotions

- ❀ E = Engagement

- ❀ R = Relationships

- ❀ M = Meaning

- ❀ A = Achievement

Let's look at each of these one by one.

POSITIVE EMOTIONS

We know through positive psychology that feeling and connecting with positive emotions is likely to increase overall well-being. There are lots of ways to encourage more positive emotions. One route is by adopting an attitude of gratitude or taking part in hobbies that bring you joy and a sense of gusto. The point here is that you are making a conscious effort to experience positivity and engage in enjoyable activities.

JOURNAL PROMPT

Increasing Positive Emotions

What am I grateful for? What activities lift my mood? What movies, songs, poems, or books make me feel good?

ENGAGEMENT

Have you ever experienced a flow state? It could be that wonderful feeling where you're completely engaged with a task and all of a sudden you look up and discover that three hours have flown by. Or maybe you move through your day with ease and grace and just generally feel good and connected with wherever you are. It could also be the feeling of getting into bed at the end of the day with a smile.

A key to being engaged is doing things that align with your interests and your aptitude. Seligman and his partner, Dr. Christopher Peterson of the University of Michigan, conducted a three-year research project where they traveled around the world developing a system of twenty-four of the most common character strengths. From there, they created a character strength assessment, a quiz to discover your leading strengths. For many years in my spiritual coaching and retreat travel business, I required my clients to take the VIA Character Strengths Survey. It's free and only takes about ten minutes to complete, it offers guidance on how to live an engaged life, and it provides a strong foundation on how each strength increases well-being, as detailed in Peterson and Seligman's 2004 book *Character Strengths and Virtues*. (Note: I am not affiliated with viacharacter. org; I'm simply an enthusiastic supporter of their product.)

Once you take the test, you can then schedule in activities that will nurture your top strengths. For example, my top strength is appreciation of beauty and excellence. This is easy to nurture when I am traveling, regularly in a state of awe, and appreciating the local food, art, and people. However, when I am back home in my normal routine, it is essential that I plan outings to museums, gardens, and parks, or schedule a nourishing coffee date, to stay connected to my top strength.

Top character strengths I see amongst my clients are oftentimes in curiosity and love of learning. So often my students in my certification and coaching programs join because they hunger to know more. One of my clients, Alexis, had a successful career as a nurse. She was called to nursing as she believed it was the best way to help people and leave the world a better place. Once she started her career path, she enjoyed the moments when she could support her patients. But after several years in the field, she felt truly burned out by the work and limited in the ways she wanted to support her patients. She wanted to share the benefits of meditation and encourage people to think more deeply about their lives. This hunger brought her into my world. Once she took the VCA, she realized that she needed to live a life where she was continuously learning about her interests. She first joined a spiritual group coaching course, where she sunk her teeth into diverse Eastern and Western spiritual themes and then took the next step to learn meditation and spiritual psychology in my certification. This led her to living a happier and more fulfilling life. She even gets to weave in her new learnings at her job! She continues to join courses and study themes that expand her curiosity.

JOURNAL PROMPT

Encouraging Engagement

What does a flow state look like for me? What are my top three character strengths? What could I do to engage these strengths more?

RELATIONSHIPS

When you are seeking a life of happiness, having positive, uplifting relationships and social connections is transformational. Having a community of like-minded peers will increase your well-being. When I share this concept with companies, I comment on how important it is to have clubs for employees to take part in. Whether it's a runners club, a book club, a new moms club, or a Mindfulness Mondays club, joining a group that's rooted in shared interests can foster new relationships and deeper connections. Are there any activities you're currently doing where you're taking an active role by welcoming in like-minded relationships? You don't need to have everything in common—just having this one interest can be enough to kick off a new friendship.

As I was on my spiritual journey and looking to connect with like-minded people, I noticed that some people outside of my friend group commented on content I was posting on social media. I paid attention to people who asked questions about yoga and meditation. I paid attention to people who loved the spiritual quotes I shared, who followed the same spiritual teachers I did, and who commented on the delicious bone broth recipe I cooked. Over time, realizing we were all on the same path, I fostered connections with these people. All it took was awareness and the desire to create a more spirituality-aligned friendship group.

So many of us have felt alone as we walk our spiritual path. Yet there are people you know who desire this connection, too. I felt happier when I was having intimate spiritual conversations with those around me. I noticed that I had to be an active participant in my own life and invite in the community I desired. This was easy to do in Bali, where almost everyone ate healthfully, went to yoga classes, and took part in breathwork or ecstatic dance—but the work was creating this community back home in Chicago.

I started hosting women's circles with one of my friends where we would share about our lives, the obstacles we were facing, and what we were manifesting. I now call these circles CounSOULS. This is a way to bring meaning to our lives as we connect with our inner guides in the company of other people who are also on the spiritual path. Can you imagine wanting to start your own circle? If so, who would you want to invite? (We'll talk more about CounSOULS in Chapter 13.)

Another great way to meet new friends is through friend matchmaking. I love this concept, and in Yiddish we actually have a word for this: *shidduch.*

Do you have any friends you could ask for introductions to someone with whom you might get along? Do you have any friends you can set up? I always love being able to connect other people and take a lot of pride when a new relationship takes off!

Finally, while meeting new people and growing new social circles to reflect your current interests, don't forget to nurture those stable, long-standing relationships too. For example, maybe you're still close with your best friends from fifth grade even though your lives have taken you across the country from each other and you've started families of your own. Maybe you still reminisce about the great friendships you made during a summer internship or camp and wonder if you should try to reach out. Having people in our lives who have known us a long time is grounding. While we're always changing and evolving, it's nice to have a connection with someone who knew us way back when (when it makes sense to keep them in our lives). Consider which of those relationships are worth preserving and tending to.

JOURNAL PROMPT

Strengthening Relationships

Is there a class, workshop, or event I can sign up for where most people are interested in what I'm interested in? Is there someone in my life who asks me questions that make me feel seen? Are there any connections

I can make between like-minded people I know? Are any of my friendships in need of nurturing? Do I want to start creating a monthly group CounSOUL?

MEANING

One of my favorite books is *Man's Search for Meaning* by Dr. Viktor Frankl. The first half of the book is his memoir sharing his experience in the Auschwitz concentration camp during the Holocaust. Frankl shares that not even Nazis can take away the beauty of the sun rising and setting in the sky. The second half of the book contains his teachings of Logotherapy, a type of therapy explaining how essential it is to have meaning in your life.

Some people find meaning in being a caregiver to their children or tending to their animals, loved ones, or garden. Others find a charity they align with and dedicate their time to that cause. And some of us are lucky enough to derive meaning from our career.

So often on the self-development path, people ask me about their purpose and how to unlock their purpose. I believe it is clearer to work with meaning and legacy energy, as these two themes will root you in action for how you want to live day to day. *Legacy energy* is what I call connecting to the reason you are here during this moment in time on planet Earth. Connecting to your legacy energy means paying attention to your natural strengths and being clear on how you want to make an impact while you're here in this lifetime. What nourishes and excites you? As you dive into the exercises in this book and strengthen your relationship with your inner guru, you will experience moments when you think, *Ah, yes! This I enjoy. I'm good at it, and it feels good, too!* This is legacy energy, and we'll explore this topic more in Chapter 9.

JOURNAL PROMPT

Exploring Meaning and Legacy Energy

Where do I find meaning in my life? Is there a cause or issue I'd like to learn more about? Is there someone in my life who might need my help? By supporting them, could I feel more connected to my legacy energy?

ACHIEVEMENT

Achievement means leveling up in your life. It signals that you're not just keeping pace, you're making positive progress forward. And even if your progress is more crisscrossed and zig-zagged than linear, taking stock of your wins, big or small, adds up over time and leads to massive growth.

In a corporate setting, achievement might mean getting that promotion with increased flexibility and more money. It could mean formal recognition for your contribution on a successful project, or an invitation to work on an exciting brand-new team. Achievement can also mean accomplishing personal goals, like running a 10K, writing a book, starting a podcast, learning to ski, consistently doing your laundry, or reaching a new level of financial abundance in your business. Spiritual achievement may look like staying calm during a conflict, or reaching a serene state of inner peace during meditation.

What does achievement mean to you? Are you a goal-oriented person? Or are you more of a vague dreamer? One of the keys to achieving anything is having a concrete, measurable goal in mind. For example, I have many clients looking to "become more mindful." What does that look like? Maybe it's maintaining a meditation streak for forty days. Maybe it's consistently taking fifteen seconds to think before responding to a tough question.

JOURNAL PROMPT

Assessing Achievement

What are three goals I have for myself? What is one step I could take today or this week to make some progress toward realizing these goals?

MARK YOUR CALENDAR

Once you become clear on how the PERMA model can support happiness in your day-to-day life, schedule it. These practices work only if you make time for them. Take out your calendar now.

* ❋ Schedule time to start a new book you're excited about, go on a bike ride with a friend, check out a new yoga studio, or listen to a new album you've heard about.

* ❋ Take part in activities that are aligned with your strengths.

- 🌼 Set up coffee dates to deepen relationships.

- 🌼 Create moments of meaning through volunteer work or service-based activities.

- 🌼 Establish a route toward your desired goals and feeling-states.

SEASONS FOR INTEGRATION AND SEASONS FOR GROWTH

In the Western world, we tend to champion pushing, hustle, and financial success and minimize the importance of rest, repair, slowing down, and presence. As a result of this imbalance, we often slip into unhealthy patterns, and our culture is rife with burnout, chronic fatigue, and stress-related health problems. By honoring the difference between growth and integration, we can see which season we are in right now and allow for moments of stillness and inner growth.

For example, many of my clients come to me once their children become more independent and wonder what is next for them. One client, Hannah, spent fifteen years raising her kids while maintaining a part-time job as a yoga teacher. Upon sharing these two seasons with her, she realized that now was the time to move into an integration season. She decided to marry her motherhood experience with her experience as a yoga instructor by supporting other mothers who wanted to introduce mindfulness techniques to their children. Her growth season was all around raising her children and learning how to best support them. Her integration season focuses on sharing what she learned as a mother to support other moms and their families.

EMBODIMENT PRACTICE: SHOULD I STAY, OR SHOULD I GROW?

Below are key indicators that can help you understand which season you're in right now. Are you implementing any of these?

Growth Season

- ✺ Traveling

- ✺ Studying

- ✺ Signing up for yoga or meditation teacher training

- ✺ Reading spiritual self-help books

- ✺ Raising children

- ✺ Listening to soul-nourishing podcasts

- ✺ Exploring food and relationships

- ✺ Being curious about language and culture

- ✺ Making new connections and relationships

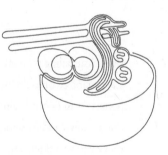

Integration Season

- ✺ Weaving in what you've learned

- ✺ Launching a program

- ❀ Writing a book

- ❀ Starting a podcast

- ❀ Getting quiet

- ❀ Sitting in stillness

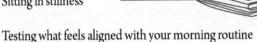

- ❀ Testing what feels aligned with your morning routine

- ❀ Showing up from a place of knowing

Look at your life through the lens of seasons. Take a moment. Are you in a growth season or an integration season right now? Seasons can last months or years. Do you want to stay in the season you're in, or do you want to shift? How can you explore the season you are in further?

BULLET JOURNAL

Bullet journaling is an intuitive practice for those of us who like to make lists to stay organized or to do brain dumps. Productivity experts love bullet journaling because it frees our brain to focus on doing what it does best—think. Writing things down reduces the cognitive load of having to remember everything. Once you've written something down, you can set it aside for the moment, then come back and prioritize your ideas.

Bullet journaling became popular during the pandemic, and it supported people in creating lists of memories that brought them joy or helped keep them on track. If you love DIY, then this is the ritual for you!

First, buy a blank notebook. You can choose one with or without lines. If you love to doodle in the margins, I suggest a notebook without lines or grids.

On the first page, write your intention for this journal. For example, "I am using this journal to attract more _____ in my life."

On the second page, write your dedication. For example, "I dedicate this journal to the version of myself who lives a joyful and nourishing life" or "I dedicate this journal to myself and my children as I become the parent (or CEO or mindful person) I know myself to be."

Skip a few pages in, and on the top of the page write the category of your first list. Here are some ideas:

- ❀ Things I am grateful for

- ❀ Activities that bring me joy

- ❀ To-do list

- ❀ Jokes that made me laugh out loud

- ❀ Books I read this year

- ❀ Books I want to read

- ❀ The coffee orders of the people I love

- ❀ Songs that make me cry in the best way

- ❀ Things I got complimented on that I may want to buy as gifts

- ❀ Recipes I want to try

- ❀ Dreams I want to remember

Allow about three to five pages for each category and add bullet points as you think of them. You could use a simple pen or colorful pencils or markers—it's up to you. Enjoy your bullet journal. Take time to make it unique to you. During your Mornings with Meaning practice, take a couple moments with your bullet journal to write down your hopes, dreams, and desires. This exercise is easy to personalize and is another tool you can use to engage with your inner guru and envision your highest possible future. Have fun!

GUIDED INTEGRATION

Happiness and living a life rooted in joy is down to a science. When we begin to look outside of ourselves to fill a void within our hearts, it is time to reflect and actively plan more positive experiences that are aligned to our strengths. The PERMA model is a transformational framework for getting clear on what will bring us everlasting joy.

- ✹ **Work with the PERMA model.** Focus on where you can add in activities that lead to joy. Engage daily with your strengths. Nurture relationships with like-minded people. Notice where in your life you find meaning and work toward a bigger goal.

- ✹ **Take the VIA Character Strengths Survey.** Once you've discovered your top strengths through this online quiz, add in some tasks, activities, and hobbies where you get to exercise these strengths.

- ✹ **Map it out.** Don't just talk about the things you want to achieve or the relationships you desire to nurture—take out your calendar and schedule them in. This means it will actually happen!

※ **Consider which season you're in right now.** There are seasons of growth and seasons to integrate what you learned. Integration is just as important to allow everything you've learned to become part of your personality and daily life.

※ **Keep a bullet journal.** Brain-dump all your brilliant ideas and running to-do lists in a bullet journal. This is a fun and creative way to list all the tasks and ideas on your mind in carefully organized categories.

CHAPTER 5

exploring emotional intelligence

*A belligerent samurai, an old Japanese tale goes, once challenged a Zen master
to explain the concept of heaven and hell. But the monk replied with scorn,
"You're nothing but a lout—I can't waste my time with the likes of you!"*

*His very honor attacked, the samurai flew into a rage and, pulling his sword from
its scabbard, yelled, "I could kill you for your impertinence."*

"That," the monk calmly replied, "is hell."

*Startled at seeing the truth in what the master pointed out about the fury that had him
in its grip, the samurai calmed down, sheathed his sword, and bowed, thanking the
monk for the insight. "And that," said the monk, "is heaven."*

*The sudden awakening of the samurai to his own agitated state illustrates the crucial
difference between being caught up in a feeling and becoming aware that you are being
swept away by it. Socrates's injunction "Know thyself" speaks to this keystone of
emotional intelligence: awareness of one's own feelings as they occur.*

—DANIEL GOLEMAN, EMOTIONAL INTELLIGENCE

We locked eyes from across the yoga shala while I sat in a meditative posture in a patch of sun. He wore a heavy cloak, perfect for warding off desert storm winds. *If he has a message for me, then he will come up and tell me,* I thought to myself, deciding to stay put and turn my face toward the sunshine. I saw him stand up and stride toward me and I got chills, feeling awkward, like maybe he'd heard my thought. *Is that even possible?*

"Hello," said this great big man whom I knew to be a shaman visiting from Europe. "My name is Leon." Leon had long, dark hair, a full beard, and wore so many layers he appeared larger than life, at least twice my size. He was also a bit dusty, like me, as a desert storm continued to blow sand all over the ashram. A shaman is a healer or teacher who has access to the spirit world or the space in between our physical realm and others. For a moment I became self-conscious, aware that my hair was on its way to accidently becoming dreadlocks and there weren't mirrors at this campsite. But then I remembered that everyone here at the desert ashram looked a little weathered.

"Hey, how's the day for you?" I asked like someone who regularly spends time with mystics (which, at the time, was not true!).

He looked me over, held my stare, and said, "I know why you are here." He paused, inhaled, and then continued. "You're traveling. You're on a quest of sorts. From America, yeah? You left a boyfriend back home, disappointed a lot of people, and decided to come here," he said with utter clarity. "How's the day for you?" he asked with a sly smile.

Before I could answer, he added, "Don't be shocked. I know a lot of things. I can even introduce you to your soulmate right now!"

Chills.

My curious eyes surveyed Shaman Leon, and I smiled at his words. "Yes . . ." I was a bit awestruck and felt silly even responding if this shaman really knew intricate details about me. "Yes . . . yes to it all—the day is wonderful, I am really enjoying this sacred journey retreat," I finally replied. I also added that my name was Erin.

He reached out, his palms facing upward, inviting me to place my hands into his. I placed my hands facedown into his large palms. We both had dirt under our nails. His hands were warm, and I relaxed.

Shaman Leon closed his eyes and took a deep inhale. I followed his lead, and we breathed together for a couple moments, the sunshine finding my face once again. It was a calming partner breathwork practice. Shaman Leon opened his eyes and kept hold of one of my hands in a loose grip. "Come on, come meet your soulmate." He walked me toward a group of people playing instruments.

Butterflies danced around my stomach. It felt like a double espresso had just hit my system. Shaman Leon left me standing around the perimeter of the group, and I watched as a handful of them tuned their instruments in preparation for a jam session. He walked up to a fully gray-haired man holding a guitar, then beckoned me to come closer with a wave.

"Erin, meet your soulmate, Eitan." Shaman Leon smiled and then walked away. Eitan laughed, shook my hand, and smiled as if this was something that had happened to him before. We connected for a moment over the strangeness of this introduction, and then I sat on a nearby chair and listened to him play his guitar with his posse. Eitan was kind and a talented musician and also much older than me. I checked in with myself, making sure I was calm in my body and self-aware in this situation. My emotions had been on high alert this whole time at this sacred journey retreat, and I needed to pause and breathe for a moment to re-regulate.

Shaman Leon did know general things about me, and Eitan was a sweet person whom I spent a few hours with and was happy meeting, but he wasn't my person, he wasn't my soulmate. It's possible that Shaman Leon saw how suggestable I was in this moment and exerted some powerful emotions my way to see how I would react. Since I was on my spiritual pilgrimage, I continuously dropped back into my body, evaluating my awareness of the situation and making sure that I was emotionally regulated and grounded. This experience showed me the importance of having a high level of emotional intelligence when walking the path of becoming your most authentic Self. Shaman Leon may have known a few things about me, but I knew me more. And my inner guru supported that connection. I trusted myself more than this shaman.

While at Columbia University, I did my master's thesis on emotional intelligence, an interesting school of science that focuses on self-awareness, emotional regulation, and mindfulness. Emotional intelligence is understanding how you feel and think while also being mindful of how the people around you feel and think. It is a practice of connecting to Self and others, specifically through social awareness, self-regulation of the nervous system, motivation, empathy, and social skill. These descriptions overlap with some yogic themes I was studying when I lived in India and Israel. There are three major themes I like to focus on with the science and understanding of emotional intelligence: self-awareness, self-regulation, and mindfulness.

SELF-AWARENESS

Self-awareness is the ability to perceive our own emotions, and the ability to be aware of other people's emotions. Self-awareness practices encourage us to think about and premeditate our actions and contemplate what other factors could bias or cloud our decision-making. Understanding your own emotions links to knowing your strengths, your weaknesses, and your drive to succeed. This is powerful in relationships, both personal and professional, so people can work together and balance their strengths.

Sigmund Freud, the founder of psychoanalysis, believed that a portion of our emotional lives is unconscious, and that self-awareness can help us recognize what lies beneath the surface and, in essence, make the unconscious conscious. An example of this looks like exploring why you may have an auto-reaction based on a sensitive question, experience, or behavior. This can also look like finding yourself facing the same obstacle over and over again and wondering why in hopes of finding a solution.

For example, my client Sophie would show up to our one-on-one coaching calls wanting to understand why she always found herself in stress-inducing situations. Either she was late on rent, or had an issue with her boss about a project, or one of her girlfriends was upset with her over something. I explained how cycles or patterns will appear when we are unaware of an underlying belief system or habit that often leads to the same result. Sophie started talking about the chaos in her house growing up. She told me about her parents and what stressful patterns were common for them. Now that Sophie had gotten herself out of the house and independent, living and working on her own, she felt that she may have needed a little bit of chaos to keep herself feeling connected to her parents. The drama in her day-to-day life would support Sophie in feeling safe and in control. She had an underlying belief system in her unconscious that a little bit of stress would keep her feeling safe. Once she became aware of that belief, she was able to release her attachment to chaos and follow a more regimented routine.

Tools to Increase Self-Awareness

❋ Take a moment to reflect.

❋ To understand the full scope of any situation, ask detailed questions.

❋ When in a decision-making situation, listen and be attentive.

❋ Check in with yourself throughout the day.

❋ If you make a mistake, own up to it. If you need to course correct, do so as soon as possible.

❋ Ask for feedback in relationships, both personal and professional.

❋ Notice how your body language reveals your inner thoughts and feelings.

MAKING DECISIONS WITH AWARENESS

Researchers suggest we make thirty-five thousand decisions a day—many within sixty minutes of waking up. Over time, our decision-making muscle gets exhausted. That is why when someone asks you where you want to go for dinner, it's difficult to choose between Mexican, Mediterranean, or Indian cuisine. It's also why making bigger life transitions can be challenging early in your self-development journey. There are so many options!

To make decisions, you need mental energy. If you're undernourished spiritually and you participate in too many activities that don't light you up, making good decisions becomes a lot harder. So, to show up for that yoga class (or that first date, or that family event) takes extra resolve. When you connect with your younger Self and your older (ideally wiser) Self, it helps you make more grounded decisions.

When I need to channel mature decisions, I imagine myself looking at the situation through my own eyes when I'm eighty. My eighty-year-old Self is my archetypal "wise woman." She has gray hair, she's wearing a red muumuu, and her breasts are swaying freely beneath the fabric. My eighty-year-old Self has spent decades working with her inner guru, so I can be assured that she's living her most authentic life. This version of myself is radically honest, and she can make decisive decisions easily.

JOURNAL PROMPTS

Imagining Your Older, Wiser Self

What does your eighty-year-old Self look like? Do you think they would overthink a conversation you had with your boss or a new friend? How would they feel about your social group? How does it feel to embody this older version of yourself?

EMBODIMENT PRACTICE:
CHOOSE AND EMBODY METHOD

When helping my clients make nonemergency decisions, and we have the time and space for them to feel into their different options, I always suggest trying this practice. It works especially well when you are indecisive and deciding between two or three options: for example, you may be debating which city to move to, which job to take, which home to purchase, etc.

Early in my business, I worked with many teenage girls. I had one client who was deciding which university would be the best fit for her, and she came to her decision by using this exercise. Here's how it works.

Pick one of your options and spend a minimum of twenty-four hours knowing that it is the best choice for you. Imagine that this is your new reality, and you're going to follow through with it. Embody what it feels like to go live in that city / choose that job / buy that home. Hop on Google Maps and discover the local coffee shops, yoga studios, and grocery stores. Imagine yourself walking through the front doors of your new company (or logging on to meet with your new colleagues and boss remotely). Take a walk in the neighborhood of the home you've just "purchased."

The next day, choose another city / job / home. Spend all day thinking about that new option. Immerse yourself in the energy of that choice in the same way you did with your first option.

Repeat this process for a third option, if you have one.

At the end of each day, write about how you felt. Pay attention to when you felt nourished, joyful, and at ease. Also notice where you felt dissonance, like maybe you couldn't be yourself, or you couldn't imagine really following through with your decision. This practice allows you to feel confident in whichever choice you ultimately make. Decision-making, when connected to your inner guru, allows you to live in alignment with your most authentic Self.

SELF-REGULATION

Self-regulation is our ability to regulate our emotions and support others' emotions in a group setting. Understanding our code of ethics and honoring it as we maintain and build relationships is the foundation of self-regulation. It inspires us to be accountable for our achievements and our downfalls, while holding others accountable for theirs.

Self-regulation is the ability to resist impulse. A famous study facilitated by Walter Mischel of Stanford, referred to as the "marshmallow study," explains how resisting impulse can lead to increased well-being. In this study, a teacher told four- and five-year-olds that they could either have one marshmallow now or they could wait until the teacher runs an errand, and when they get back, the children will receive two marshmallows. Around two-thirds of the children practiced delayed gratification and enjoyed two marshmallows after the teacher completed the twenty-minute errand. About ten years later, the researchers connected with those same kids. As adolescents, the children who had waited were more socially competent, effective, and self-assertive, and they were better at coping with the frustrations of life. The children who had opted for immediate gratification shied away from social contracts and were insecure and indecisive. They were easily upset or frustrated and thought of themselves as "bad" or unworthy.

In today's world, we want what we want, and we want it now. This research is powerful because it explains that denying yourself something, and regulating an emotional impulse, can lead you closer to your goal. Whether that means studying in a particular field for a long time, writing a novel, maintaining a long-term lifestyle shift, or starting a business, individuals who delay gratification are demonstrating what is known as a "low time preference." In other words, you choose the positive long-term outcome over the short-term pleasure. In praxeology, the study of human action, delaying consumption in order to add value to your future Self is a low time preference behavior. It is taking care of the future version of you because the goal requires time to get there.

Delaying gratification and working daily toward one specific goal or lifestyle is a great self-development strategy because books are not written in one day. A healthy life is a daily practice; it cannot be just a twenty-four-hour behavior change. Becoming an expert in a given field requires years of dedication, and some of our greatest dreams take time to build upon the skill. Many of us are not overnight success stories; we require building over time to reach that success.

If you want to see low time preference behavior in action, google the phrase "Kid's Candy Challenge" on YouTube. There are thousands of videos online of parents putting candy in front of their child (while filming them with their phone) and saying, "You can eat all the candy when I come back in a couple of minutes." In these videos children have internal dilemmas whether to eat the candy while the parent is away or not. This has become a social experiment in our modern world and is super cute to watch!

Tools to Increase Self-Regulation

- ※ Pause before reacting. Collect yourself. Then respond.

- ※ Write down your values, morals, or code of ethics. Are you living in alignment with them?

- ※ Recognize someone for a job well done.

- ※ So no to impulse buys, impulse texts, and other quick decisions that aren't in line with what you really value.

- ※ Write a letter of gratitude to someone who has supported you (aka a thank you note).

- ☀ Engage in a hard conversation with someone who has a different political stance or worldview than you do.

- ☀ Make a point to lead by example.

MINDFULNESS

Mindfulness is our ability to be calm, centered, and accepting of the present moment. It offers you the opportunity to create space between an action and a reaction. Mindfulness also decreases anxiety and stress levels, leading to a healthier life.

A 2018 study measured the effects of mindfulness programing in traditional workspaces and found that employees experienced increased empathy and stronger teamwork following the sessions. Productivity and overall workplace morale also improved. Employees surpassed their goals, felt more energized and less stressed, and they were even more present with their families at home. The benefits of mindfulness are numerous, and it's something we can all practice.

One of my favorite studies on mindfulness meditation investigates the therapeutic benefits of this practice. In 2011, a team of Harvard-affiliated researchers directed a group of participants to meditate for about twenty-seven minutes each day for eight weeks, focusing on gentle body scans and connecting to the awareness of their breath and the present moment. The researchers observed participants' brains with a magnetic resonance (MR) scan before and after their meditation immersion. Dr. Sara Lazar and her team went into the study knowing that meditation leads to a sense of peacefulness and physical relaxation, but they wanted to explore the cognitive and psychological benefits that occur after a mindfulness session. In the group that had a consistent meditation practice, researchers noticed that reductions in stress were associated with decreased gray-matter density in the amygdala, a small, almond-shaped part of the brain that governs emotions and plays an important role in anxiety and stress. The researchers also noticed an increase in gray matter in the hippocampus, which oversees learning, self-awareness, and memory. Through meditation and mindfulness practices, the study says, the brain can change, and well-being can increase.

Tools to Increase Mindfulness

* Slow down. Concentrate on completing one task at a time.

* Offer your full attention to the present moment and accept how you feel without judgment.

* Notice your breath right now. How does your inhale and exhale feel in your body?

* Check in. Practice returning to the present moment throughout your day.

* Try a guided meditation, such as the Rainbow Meditation below.

RAINBOW MEDITATION

This meditation is great for beginner meditators or children and is even a powerful tool for seasoned meditators. This is a calming practice that guides you into a relaxing and peaceful state using the colors of the rainbow. It can also be used as a sleep meditation if you are experiencing insomnia.

To start, lie down in savasana (on your back) or settle into a seated posture. Make sure that if you choose to lie down, you're taking up space on the floor by opening your arms and legs, feeling supported by the earth. This is symbolic of taking up space in your life.

Close your eyes. Connect with your breath, inhaling and exhaling gently to clear and ground yourself. Take a moment to feel into your body. Is this the first time you've been still today?

On your next inhale, picture the color red. Red lies at the base of the tail-bone. Exhale. Take your time.

On your next inhale, picture the color orange. Orange lies at the hips. Exhale.

On the next inhale, picture the color yellow. Yellow lies at the navel. Exhale.

On your next inhale, picture the color green. Green lies at the heart. Exhale.

On your next inhale, picture the color blue. Blue lies at the throat. Exhale.

On your next inhale, picture the color indigo. Indigo lies at the third-eye center, between the eyebrows. Exhale.

On your next inhale, picture the color violet. Violet lies at the crown (the top of the head). Exhale.

Lie down if you are not already doing so, allowing yourself to absorb the practice. Visualize all the colors of the rainbow activating, starting at the base of the tailbone and going all the way to the top of your head. Breathe.

This meditation can be as short as five minutes or as long as twenty minutes. Listen to your inner guru and allow yourself to take many inhales and exhales between each color if desired. It will guide you on the time you need.

SLOWING DOWN

I noticed early in my spiritual journey that I was always in a hurry—in a hurry to wake up, in a hurry to go for a run, in a hurry to get home to eat something, in a hurry to get to work, in a hurry to finish work—it was go, go, go, from morning until bedtime. I was even sometimes in a hurry to move through my meditation or spiritual practices. All this hurrying showed me that I was under-living—I was not living in the present moment. I was allowing life to flow by without experiencing it. When you are under-living, you are out of alignment and disconnected from your inner guru and your most authentic Self.

Slow living is another tool you can use to regulate your nervous system. Slow living does not mean you are moving slowly—it means you are moving through your day with meaning and connection. Slow living is not about how much you got done in a day, but about how you felt along the way. Living slowly feels good on the inside.

For example, I used to be the type of host who cleans dishes the second everyone is done eating; however, when I got into slow living, I realized that if I'm off in the kitchen doing dishes, I'm missing valuable time connecting with my guests. The dishes don't need to be cleaned this second—they can wait an hour or until everyone leaves.

Slow living looks like going out of your way to change and put on comfy clothes. Wouldn't your beautiful and nourishing lunch taste so much better if you took off your bra and put on your comfiest muumuu? Wouldn't you have more fun doing housework if you turned on a podcast or practiced lower belly breathing while completing chores? Will that proposal you need to write be more joyful if you pause and made yourself a warm drink? Find ways to enjoy every moment as much as possible, and move at a calmer, slower pace. The hope is a more relaxed nervous system, a less hurried life, and presence as you fully live.

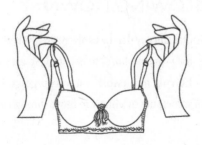

EMBODIMENT PRACTICE: SLOW LIVING

Implement slow living into your daily life by practicing some of these ideas:

- ❋ Set out time to have your morning cup of tea or coffee by yourself in silence or with a loved one.

- ❋ Watch the sun set or rise.

- ❋ Take a walk in the morning for pleasure rather than exercise.

- ❋ Notice which chores light you up and which feel draining.

- ❋ Spend less time on social media.

- ❋ Organize your social and work calendars so you don't have too much scheduled on one specific day.

- ❋ Ask for help when life is feeling too full.

- ❋ Notice your breath.

- ❋ Sit on your front porch or balcony (or go to the park) and observe the world around you.

- ❋ Take a bath or a long shower.

- ❋ Sunbathe for a few minutes if you can.

- ❋ Allow yourself to be imperfect and messy now and then.

If you're thinking that you have way too much to do as it is and you can't possibly slow down, I'd encourage you to take a brief pause and assess what must be done versus what would be nice to get done. Oftentimes, we have things on our plate that simply don't belong there. This is a great time to practice delay, delegate, and delete. Which tasks can be put off or delayed for another day? What could you delegate to a partner or contract worker? What is filling your schedule that you could simply skip altogether? A big part of discovering your authentic Self is making room for your true desires to come through and allow yourself to lessen your daily load.

DEFINE YOUR BIG BELIEFS

Something I hear about from my clients all the time is their fear that someone is upset with them. I had one client, Sarah, explain that her friend hadn't texted her back in a few days and she was afraid she was mad at her. Another client, Marcy, heard from her boss that she needed to speak to her at the end of the day. Marcy automatically assumed that she'd done something wrong and her boss was upset with her. In reality, Sarah's friend was out of the country and not answering her phone. And Marcy's boss wanted only to clarify a few details with her before a big project presentation. These anxiety-producing stories are what Brené Brown calls "the story I am making up."

The story we play in our heads can sometimes be a sort of worst-case scenario, when in the real world it is nothing "bad" at all. When we honor our emotional intelligence practices, we can reground and regulate ourselves emotionally before spiraling into a fear-based thought cycle.

An important question I ask my clients when these fear-based obstacles present themselves is: *What is the big belief here?*

Big belief means the actual, zoomed out, fear-based thought that requires self-awareness. For example, Sara was afraid that her friend was mad at her because she wasn't texting back. But when we zoomed out, we discovered that

Sarah's big belief—her bigger, more general fear—was a feeling of being left behind or abandoned, a story she made up after a former friend dropped her without any explanation. This showed us where the healing needed to happen and where the thought patterns need to shift for Sarah so she could come back into alignment.

We uncovered that Marcy's big belief was that she was not smart and that her boss was going to "find out" or "catch her." Marcy had worked her way up the corporate ladder and now led a large team at a successful advertising agency. But she'd struggled to get decent grades in high school and didn't perform very well on standardized tests, and the school system had taught her that she was "average." Marcy and I focused on understanding how her strengths and talents fit well with her current job. In fact, Marcy's innate work habits and creativity had served her well (something the modern-day school system frequently doesn't capture, and a problem a lot of my clients face, unfortunately). So, we rewrote Marcy's narrative. By focusing on her big belief—the root cause of her anxiety—we were able to notice where this played out in her life and insert positive mantras to remind her of her strengths. One mantra that supported her was, "I see the world uniquely. I am a creative genius!" This allowed her to reclaim her power at work.

This is a continual practice of self-awareness and curiosity. When you are texting with someone and you don't hear back right away, do you assume their lack of response has to do with you personally, or do you think they just got distracted or are busy? What behavior(s) do you keep repeating that are not in alignment with your desires? For example, I had a client who would download the dating apps, connect with people, but never show up for the first date because her big belief was that she would never find her beloved even though she deeply desired a romantic partnership. Once she identified the limiting belief, she realized her consistent self-sabotaging behavior. We decided that for her next date she would meet this potential suitor at a café right next to her apartment so it would be incredibly convenient for her to walk over. I also asked her about some other women in her life who struggled with dating and now had successful, inspiring romantic relationships. She had many to reference. Once she noticed that it was possible for other people in her life and made it easy for herself to show up, she began successfully dating, which led to meeting her beloved.

Defining your big beliefs is another way to become aware of the storylines you've created that could be blocking you from living your fullest and most embodied life. When we react or get defensive, it can oftentimes be a programming or trigger response based on a deeper big belief. Take note and be gentle with the themes that unfold. The best part is that once you become clear on your big beliefs, you can begin to write a new story.

GUIDED INTEGRATION

Emotional intelligence is understanding how you feel and think while also being mindful of how the people around you feel and think. Working on self-awareness, self-regulation, and mindfulness can help strengthen your relationships with yourself and others. By becoming more aware and defining the big beliefs behind your fears, you have the tools to increase your well-being.

- ❀ **Pay attention.** Self-awareness brings you to the present moment and will support you with clear decision-making.

- ❀ **Delay gratification?** Self-regulation shows us that when we have low time preference and delay immediate gratification, it can lead to more success, wellness, and fulfillment long term.

- ※ **Inhale and exhale.** Mindfulness is a power tool to decrease stress and increase energy. Start practicing with a gentle body scan and the Rainbow Meditation. Keep the practice long term to reap the benefits.

- ※ **Make decisions from a place of embodiment.** When it comes to decision fatigue and deciding which choice will lead to your highest possible timeline, try the Choose and Embody method. This practice encourages you to deeply embody the possibilities you have, allowing you to make clear and confident choices.

- ※ **Identify your big beliefs.** Once you become clear on a limiting belief, you can move past it. Pay attention to themes that occur repeatedly that leave you in an anxious state, and ask yourself, I wonder what the big belief is behind that? Work with facts and mantras to reclaim your power.

CHAPTER 6

manifesting your highest soulmate

One is loved because one is loved. No reason is needed for loving.

—PAULO COELHO, THE ALCHEMIST

You are worthy to be loved by your highest possible soulmate.

You are worthy to be loved by your current romantic partner.

You are worthy to be loved by yourself as you navigate diverse romantic experiences.

Wherever you are on your romantic journey, it's important to take stock of what you value in a partner and how you want to feel in romantic partnership.

If you desire to call in, attract, and manifest your highest possible romantic partner, then this is the chapter for you. If you are already partnered or thriving as a solo freebird, please do not skip this section, as this chapter can offer guidance on how you can manifest other relationships, desires, and experiences in your life.

Maybe you're someone who has a "type" but things never seem to work out; maybe you say you simply don't have time to meet a bunch of people and go on a bunch of dates that you believe won't work out anyway. I am here to tell you that if you put conscious effort into manifesting your desires, you will attract more love and more of what your heart yearns for into your life.

Six years ago, I was seeking a partner who would travel the world with me and eventually bring life into the world alongside me. Someone who would develop with me spiritually and who also had their own style of creativity and gusto for life. I wanted to be with someone who was looking to be their best Self and who would inspire me to do the same. And I found it all in my soulmate, Jon. This is the process that guided me, and many of my other clients, to finding their beloveds.

nothing can stop you

MY JOURNEY TO JON

"Hi, Erbish. Dad and I just left the Gordon family wedding," Mom told me over the phone as they drove from Michigan back to Chicago. "Can you make sure Murphy is fed and take him on a walk?"

"Yes, of course," I said. "How was the wedding?" I was half paying attention to a show I was watching while cuddling with our family dog, one of the greatest loves of my life.

"The wedding was great. The air-conditioning went out and it was hot, but a fun wedding and a great band! And you know what? That Jon put on a show." Mom was referring to the groom's younger brother. "Erin, I think you would like him. He's warm, adventurous, and he lived in Israel in college. You two would hit it off!"

I rolled my eyes. "Mom. He's two grades younger than me—there's no way. AND I am moving to India in a few weeks!" I sassed her and sent a lot of "no one understands me" energy. How could she say such a wild thing? I was a free-spirited nomad, a super-spiritual yogi, and this boy was from my hometown. No way would we ever get along. (My ego knew no bounds.)

Then, as I hung up the phone, I thought, *Mom is cool. Mom wouldn't have just said that to say it.* As the saying goes, "Mom is always right."

August 2016

The hardwood floor in my Upper West Side apartment was the only relief from the heat. I lay on the cold floor, allowing the change in temperature to balance the heat in my body. It was so fucking hot. I was in New York for my summer term at Columbia University and decided that today I was going to manifest my soulmate.

So, I got up and created the scene. I lit a candle, put on a flowy dress from India, and wrapped myself in a shawl from Israel, honoring and symbolizing the journey that had led me to this point. I sat down, breathed into the depths of my

lower belly, and watched the sun setting outside my window. At the suggestion of a classmate, a healer, I wrote down what I was calling in.

I desired my soulmate—my highest romantic partner, the father to my future children—to come to me. This message replayed in my mind: "May our love inspire the world. May our love inspire the world. May our love inspire the world." I used the blank side of a mandala coloring book to write down my order to the Universe.

I connected with my inner guru, breathing into a quiet part of myself, allowing intuition to guide me. Once grounded, I called in all my ancestors and the ancestors of my soulmate, asking them to support my ceremony. I invited in only the highest light of my ancestors, leaving no invitation to any energy besides the clearest and kindest energies. Peacefully, I took a handful of breaths and pictured golden, braided roots at the base of my tailbone, keeping me rooted in the here and now. On my next inhale, I sat in the feeling of being present with my beloved, of being in his energy. My body had a physical reaction of feeling warm, joyful, and I relaxed deeper. I allowed my imagination to drift— *What would a day look like with my beloved?*

I got clear on all my feeling-states: waking up to my King in the bed beside me. Drinking coffee together. Turning toward each other in a fetal pose after a sweaty yoga class. Going on a love walk, hand in hand. Running mundane

nothing can stop you

errands and being silly in the grocery store. Enjoying each other's company during a delayed flight. Decompressing on the couch after spending hours talking about ideas.

The deeper I got into my ceremony, the more emotions I felt. I was so moved by my vision for my life with this partner, I started to tear up. I felt in my inner being that this relationship would be of the highest good for all. If I am feeling loved, secure, and held, I can show up for myself and my work in a bigger, aligned way. I picked up some colored pencils and my worksheet. While honoring my lower belly breaths, I wrote down all my feeling-states. *What would it feel like to be with this person?*

Here's the fun part of this ceremony. These feeling-states only needed to make sense to me. So, I wrote in my love language metaphors unique to the love I was calling in. How being with my beloved felt like getting free dessert at my favorite restaurant or getting picked up from the airport after a work trip away. Responding to him in Hebrew instead of in English. Falling asleep after sunset and waking up well rested at dawn. Smelling fresh-cut grass on a cozy, overcast day. I wrote my heart out, writing in a language only I would understand, weaving in intricate details. Laughing when his chest hair got mussed up, kissing his full lips, rubbing my face against his beard, feeling safe under his wingspan. These details were focused on feeling-states, and accompanied the physical characteristics I desired in my beloved.

I filled the whole page, feeling closer to my beloved than ever before. I read over everything and edited it. The details were all there. While staying connected to my breath and remembering the connection to my ancestors, I closed out the practice with gratitude. Gratitude for the support of my lineage and those who watch over me. Gratitude for taking the time to get clear on whom I was calling in and for the presence of my beloved's energy. Also, overwhelming appreciation for myself, for showing up for the work and taking the time to be vulnerable with myself. *Yes, life is wonderful now,* I thought. And with my beloved I felt how good it could truly get, and I for sure had the audacity to pursue that love.

Still connected to my breath, I folded up the piece of paper and hid it among my books and organized chaos. I closed out the ceremony with a sacred mantra. I prepared myself for sleep. I blew out the candle to signify the end of the ceremony. I went to bed.

Patience was going to be a key player here, and I knew from my ceremony that I could wait and be patient because the love coming my way was worth it. I also worked with the mantra *I trust the timing of my life.* My daily homework was to take parts of this ceremony, the feelings of being with my beloved, and combine them with a vision of a specific moment in time of us being together. This is called Snapshot Manifestation.

September 2017

"Alright, Erin, it's finalized! Sweet home, Chicago," my brother, Matthew, said. I hung up the phone, elated by this news. He and his then fiancé, now wife, were moving back to Chicago. I was so happy! My siblings and I hadn't lived in the same place for a long time.

I was wearing a modest green dress, waiting for Mom to be ready as we headed to our synagogue for Rosh Hashanah, the Jewish new year. It's a happy time. I get to see my best friends and eat my favorite foods with my family. I love my synagogue, my rabbi, and the people I only see this time of year. No matter where someone lives, it is the most special time in our Jewish community— everyone comes home and celebrates together.

Dad debated: Should he drop us off at the front of our synagogue, or did we want to walk with him from our parking spot ten blocks away? I opted to walk with him, enjoying the fall weather. Our walk to the synagogue was part of the experience for me. We talked about how excited we were to have Matthew back in Chicago.

While walking into the temple, I saw many of our closest family friends. I saw my lifelong best friend, Pamela, and told her the exciting news. "Matthew is moving back!" I saw our family friends and shared the joyous news with them. Before sitting down, I noticed our family friends, the Gordons. I walked up to Mindy, the mother, saying "*Shana tova*" ("Happy New Year"). "Great news," I said. "Matthew is moving back!"

"That's wonderful!" Mindy said. "And Erin, just so you know, Jon is single." She gave me a warm smile, with a bit of a Jewish-mother-matchmaking, stirring-the-pot kind of vibe.

I was a bit shocked and ended up smiling in response, unsure how to respond. Mom had shared a similar sentiment two years earlier. I sat down with my family in our designated seats. I looked over toward the Gordons and saw Jon standing next to his brother, eyes closed, immersed in the Torah service. *How pious* . . . I thought. And also . . . *Wow, what a big, beautiful, hairy man!* I felt God giving me a wink.

Weeks went by. I was briefly dating someone and could feel the breakup en route. But more than anything, I could feel my beloved nearby. I sat in the feeling-state of my ceremony every day and meditated. I knew that my sacred relationship was so near. And I found myself thinking about Jon and the conspiring comments of Jewish mothers. So, I made a wish. If it is meant to be, it will be. I also took a gentle aligned action, and I opened up Facebook and sent Jon a friend request.

November 2017

"Hey, what's up?"

I noticed the notification before bed. I must have silenced them at some point and didn't realize that the message has been sitting there all day. It was from Jon. He'd slid into my DMs. And I loved it!

"I just got back from a conference in Atlanta," I messaged back. "I'm looking forward to Thanksgiving with family."

Jon responded immediately. "I'm in Africa, traveling through Morocco, and then meeting up with a friend in Uganda and we are traveling together to Kenya."

Jon shared some beautiful insights on his travels, sent me many pictures, asked me detailed questions, always replied to my responses immediately, and even doubled-messaged me. Two weeks later, when he was back in the US, we met for a dinner date. He wanted to take me to a Thai restaurant he'd heard was authentic. As Divine would have it, it is my favorite restaurant ever. I was freshly single and excited!

December 2017

I sat at the Thai restaurant on Chicago Avenue wearing my yoga clothes. I'd just taught a meditation workshop in the suburbs, and it was important to me to show up as myself, in my comfiest clothes, still in the energy of my meditation workshop.

I trusted God in this moment. A part of my ego was telling me, *Erin, he's younger than you. He's from your hometown. There's no way he is going to understand your soul....* A tap on my right shoulder interrupted that negative thought, and a gorgeous, bearded man said "Hi" and sat down across from me. And there he was: the feeling-states I had embodied during my manifestation ceremony, my beloved. He was everything I'd been calling in my meditations.

My beloved, in living, physical form. My dream partner. I felt like I was in the presence of the father of my children, my spiritual life partner, the King of my heart.

We were together every day until I led a trip to Israel in mid-December 2017. I got back in time for Christmas, when my whole family went to Florida to celebrate my grandparents' fiftieth wedding anniversary. Jon happened to be there, too—divine timing, as that was always his original plan—and he met everyone I love.

I went back to Israel to lead another trip, and he picked me up from the airport in January 2018. We moved in together a few weeks later. We booked one-way tickets to Bangkok a few months later and backpacked through Asia in the summer of 2018 and got engaged in March 2019. We had a small wedding in August 2020 in the back yard of our synagogue overlooking Lake Michigan due to the pandemic, and then a big wedding the following August. Our nomadic life together feels like a string of honeymoons.

ENDING ONE CHAPTER
TO BEGIN A NEW ONE

All my past relationships led me to Jon. I had one long-term relationship before Jon. We met during my junior year of college, while studying in Florence, Italy, and dated on and off for five years. It was a healthy relationship, one born from close friendship and respect. However, my inner guru communicated with me often, especially in the middle of the night, telling me that he wasn't my forever partner. It took gusto and trust in myself to walk away from a good thing. We don't talk about this enough: it takes confidence and strength to leave something good because we know, in our inner being, that something more magical, connected to God, of the "highest possible timeline," is coming for us, if we make space for it in our lives. Making space requires breaking up and creating emotional room for another possible soulmate to enter.

There is a spiritual proverb that I reference often in my coaching sessions with clients: *Once you know, you can never unknow.* Once you know, at your core, that you don't feel seen in a romantic partnership, you can never unknow that. It doesn't matter if the sex is good or if you both believe in the same God or live in the same place. Once you know, your job is to honor the knowing and take aligned action. That sometimes means taking radical action—like breaking up with your current partner, moving cities, being vulnerable, or taking a risk and asking someone out. Trust in your inner guru's knowing, and then take action. The opposite is also true. This knowing can also be deeply positive, like an inner knowing that your good friend from growing up, who always felt like home, is the exact person you need to be dating right now. Pay attention and source from feeling-states.

EMBODIMENT EXERCISE:
EXPLORING FEELING-STATES

We've talked a bit already about feeling-states; this next practice will help you work with feeling-states while manifesting. To recap, feeling-states are emotional states in which you are filled up with the aliveness of your senses or explaining something using a metaphor that feels similar to what you are calling in or explaining. When you enter a feeling-state, you mimic *how you would feel "if"*—if you were in a loving partnership and your beloved cooked you a special meal; if you were a bestselling author and as you reach to pay for your coffee at your local coffee shop the barista says, "It's on the house" because your book was so impactful for them; if you walked into your boss's office and there was a gorgeous bouquet of flowers for you to celebrate your big promotion, etc. The embodiment of the feeling-state is crucial in calling in your beloved (or anything you deeply desire, really). When you are clear on the feeling, you will notice moments in your life when that feeling presents itself, aligning you with your highest possible timeline and most authentic path.

Feeling-states are a unique personal language.

Sometimes our language limits us and we lack the needed words to express what we are calling in. Use symbols, colors, and metaphors during your feeling-state manifestation ceremonies. Remember, you can call in physical attributes you desire in your beloved via feeling-states as well. For example, imagine the feeling-state you'd experience when you borrow your beloved's sweatshirt and how cozy and safe you feel in it.

JOURNAL PROMPT

Feeling into Feeling-States

Take a moment to list some of the feeling-states you're calling in.

EMBODIMENT EXERCISE: SPIRIT BABIES

If you are calling in your beloved and you hope to raise children together, take a moment during your ceremony to connect with your spirit babies. Spirit babies are the souls of your children, either yet to be birthed, or connected to you through adoption (or any route via which a child could end up in your care). I am the child of an adopted mother. My father's family has a "yours, mine, and ours" story. So, remember, your children do not need to come from your body or your bloodline. Your babies will find you. You may become a parent in the traditional sense, through birthing a child, or you may take another miraculous route. I pray you can trust and relax into your inner knowing that your spirit babies will always find you.

Connect with your spirit baby. While in meditation, ask your spirit baby these questions:

✸ What feeling-states come forth when you are with me/my partner?

✸ What can I do to become clearer on the steps I need to take to meet/ connect with my beloved?

※ How do you want to feel in your relationship with the soulmate I am calling in, your future parent?

※ Is there anything else I need to know?

Once you feel you've reached a stopping point, thank your spirit baby and say goodbye for now. If there are other spirit babies you wish to meet, you can call on another now and repeat the questions above with them too.

When you've finished, close your ceremony by spending a few minutes in quiet meditation and then slowly return to your space and your body. Know that you can come back to this space whenever you wish.

If you love this topic and want to learn more, I suggest checking out clairvoyant medium Walter Makichen's transformational book *Spirit Babies: How to Communicate with the Child You're Meant to Have.*

SNAPSHOT MANIFESTATION

Okay, y'all. This is the holy grail of manifestation practices. If you are calling in multiple desires at once, including your soulmate, then this is the practice for you!

This is a life-changing, miracle-enhancing manifestation that will get you closer to all your deepest desires and dreams and attract people into your life whom you resonate with deeply. If you are already with your beloved, that is such a win for all of us, and I'm truly happy for you! This manifestation will support you in calling in other desires, too. You will know where to edit accordingly based on the tutorial below.

To start, sit in a comfortable posture. Bring yourself close energetically, which means honoring your rawness and realness, all layers of you. Feel into your own presence, your own essence. Take a few minutes to arrive through gentle breathing. Picture golden, braided roots at the base of your tailbone, moving through the floor, into the ground and connecting to the earth's core. You are grounded, centered, and present. Take a moment to envision this connection. You are rooted in the physical world.

Picture an event you have coming up within the next six to eighteen months. It is important to choose an event that is planted on your calendar and will happen with or without you—for example, a wedding, a religious milestone, or a family trip. It cannot be something hypothetical, like "When my family comes to visit me sometime…" or "When I achieve this goal or have an imaginary party …" Choose a set-in-stone event that is going to happen no matter what.

Get a clear vision of the event in your mind. What are you wearing? How do you look and feel? Who is there with you? Hold that snapshot in your mind. Connect to the feeling of having all you desire at this one given moment. You can play out any scenario that suits you—maybe you run into a past client who wants to run an exciting new business idea past you, or you meet a superfan who loved your last art show. Details, details, details! Maybe someone compliments your dress, and you tell them that you got it on a recent European adventure!

Focus on the feeling-states that come up for you in this one snapshot in time: everything you desire is happening. Maybe you check your phone and there's an email congratulating you on your promotion. Perhaps you open up social media and your blog has gone viral. Maybe you place your hand on your belly and feel thrilled to be pregnant. Maybe you are at an event with your beloved, holding their hand, feeling loved and at peace. Pay attention to your energy at this moment in time and feel into as many details as possible.

Breathe into your snapshot for a couple minutes. Then come back into your space with a couple deep breaths. Picture the golden, braided roots at the base of your tailbone. You are grounded. Centered. Present. Picture the connection.

Return to this feeling and vision of your Snapshot Manifestation daily. If your vision feels far off, be gentle with yourself. Remember, your desires are unique to you and exist for a reason as a strong suggestion from the Universe of what is in union with your authentic Self. In his bestselling novel *The Alchemist,* Paulo Coelho says, "Your desires exist for a reason. It is your soul mission on this earth." Your desires are unique to you, your legacy energy, your passion, and your calling in this life. Pursue them. Remember, your desires are also for the highest good of all. When you pursue your heart's wishes, it's a win-win.

EMBODIMENT PRACTICE: ALIGNED ACTION

Snapshot Manifestation does four things:

It offers course correction. If your vision is nothing close to what your life looks like now, this is your wake-up call. Become aware. Starting today, take massive actions on your dreams. Write down any clear differences between your Snapshot Manifestation and your current day-to-day life.

It informs the present moment and helps with decision-making. For example, if you see yourself as a published author, or in a loving partnership, or strong and toned—but you are not writing, dating (or making any effort to date), or moving your body, something needs to shift! Take out your calendar. Schedule time every day, if possible, to do the activities that will bring you into alignment with the person you are in your Snapshot Manifestation. Call these times "Soul Time" and schedule Soul Time daily (we explore this concept more in Chapter 7). For example, set aside time to write each day, go on at least one date every couple weeks, or walk or bike instead of driving your car when you can.

It allows you to dive deeper than using language alone. This feeling-based practice means you can call in many desires at once. Feeling-states are a holistic, wholesome way of envisioning what you want your life to feel like. For example, perhaps you desire coziness, but it's not just "comfy clothes on the couch" you want. You also want your romantic partner cooking pancakes in the kitchen, a fireplace heating a light-filled room, a soft jazz record playing in the background, and your children napping while you rest on the couch. Coziness embodies multiple desires in one. What strong feelings came forth for you?

It shows you what you desire in your heart. You want what you want because your soul longs for you to live your fullest life, which means going after your desires. The moment you stop judging yourself for it, pursue it, and embody that version of yourself, everything will change.

Friends, please make Snapshot Manifestation a daily practice. All you need is a couple minutes of sitting in your manifestation ceremony. Expect miracles. Once they happen, please DM me on Instagram—I'd love to hear all about your wins!

GUIDED INTEGRATION

We are all worthy of love. If you are looking to call in your highest soulmate or manifest more heart-aligned desires, taking time to get clear on the feeling-states you desire to embody will help you make your dreams a reality.

- ☀ **Remember that feeling-states are your unique language.**
  When you are becoming clear on what you desire, work with feeling-states as opposed to a checklist. Feeling-states are a unique code personalizing what it would feel like if you had the thing your heart yearns for.

- ☀ **Try Snapshot Manifestation for yourself.** This powerful manifestation practice will support you in manifesting many desires at once and in calling in your beloved. Please remember that the integration piece of Snapshot Manifestation is connecting to the feeling-state for a couple minutes every day post-ceremony.

- ☀ **Practice patience.** Finding the right person for you may take time, and the most important thing is to stay clear on the feeling-state. When you are certain of the outcome you can enjoy the journey that will lead to your beloved. Work with the mantra, "I trust the timing of my life."

- ☀ **Don't fight it—Mama is always right!** Well, maybe not always—but it is so important to pay attention to what is occurring naturally. Notice the loving suggestions from close relationships in your life, and try your best to release judgment and keep an open mind.

do the thing

*I think perfectionism is based on the obsessive belief that if you
run carefully enough, hitting each stepping-stone just right, you won't
have to die. The truth is that you will die anyway and that a lot of people
who aren't even looking at their feet are going to do a whole lot better
than you, and have a lot more fun while they're doing it.*

—ANNE LAMOTT, BIRD BY BIRD

"Ugh, I don't understand how people do it all!" a client of mine, Liza, shared while on a group coaching video call. Some of the other participants nodded in agreement, signaling that they too have felt this frustration.

We were exploring the charged topic of following our deepest dreams and the specific aligned physical action we must take for them to occur. Another one of my clients, Shantae, unmuted herself. "I want to make my dream happen, but I often wait until I feel the inspiration or until my schedule is more open or until my home is clean." She ended with a laugh because it was SO relatable to everyone on the call. The chat box reflected this with heart emojis and other icons showing their similar resonance.

A few comments got some extra "likes" in the chat box:

Liza wrote: "Or I wait until the kids are out of the house."

Shelly wrote: "Or until everything feels perfect."

Tova wrote: "Or until I don't feel so tired."

Mike wrote: "Or until I hit a specific income level."

"Erin, how do you balance it all? You've achieved so much, how do you do it?" Liza asked after reading through the comments.

The compliment was said in passing and I normally would have laughed it off, but truthfully, I have generated success in my field and have many thoughts on how others can do the same. I run a thriving business, have a loving partnership, a healthy headspace, a book deal, self-confidence, health (poo poo poo). It was also why this group of people signed up to work with me in one of my more intimate coaching programs in the first place. As their guide, it felt important to accept the compliment graciously and answer in a way that could provide massive value and bring them closer to their goals. (Women, can we please start taking the compliment without making a humbling joke?)

I took the compliment. And answered honestly.

"I'm not a perfectionist, and I don't procrastinate," I said. "I have a devoted meditation practice that has transformed my life, so I'm in a healthy head-space most days. I'm clear on what I need to do to live the life I desire. And I see my work as representative of my devotion to God and my trust in my inner guru."

Liza nodded and smiled. The rest of the call was devoted to exploring how perfection and procrastination show up in our day-to-day lives and how to over-come them.

THE MYTH OF PERFECT

One of the greatest mantras that has supported my life and business is: "Done is better than perfect." I have taken that mantra to heart. Nothing kills creativity like perfectionism. I've met many brilliant people, and some of them never did the thing they desired because of their perfectionist tendencies.

We have normalized perfectionism in society by defining people as type A. This is a hardworking, competitive category of people—maybe we even consider them to be workaholics. Perfectionists desire achievement above all—getting to first place or getting perfect scores. Many are proud to be type A personalities. Some people even write on their dating app profiles and résumés that they identify as type A—they wear the label like a badge of honor.

The term "type A" was coined by two cardiologists, Meyer Friedman and Ray Rosenman, who in 1959 published an article in the *Journal of the American Medical Association* about coronary heart disease. They observed that people with type A personality traits, which they identified as those eager to accomplish a goal or achieve as much as possible, are at higher risk for heart disease because they live more stress-induced lives. This all turned out to be bunk. Researchers later revealed that their studies were sponsored by the tobacco industry, which had been hoping to shift the blame of diseases from smoking to type A personality behaviors. Still, the term stuck, and we use it today to define people who are high achievers and who seem to thrive on stress.

Perfectionism is a learned behavior.

When a child receives good grades in school or keeps their bedroom tidy, their parent may compliment their good behavior and achievements. Maybe this child is also an athlete, can run a mile faster than their classmates, and gets rewarded for their athletic achievements. Over time, this child will seek high achievement in order to receive praise every time they do something. They learn to be perfect (or try to be) in everything they do. The intrinsic satisfaction of figuring something out on your own; experimenting and making mistakes; overcoming obstacles, no matter how long it takes—all of these important and character-building experiences are diminished when the focus is on looking or seeming perfect, and on receiving outside validation and recognition of that perfection.

In David Bayles's and Ted Orland's book *Art & Fear*, the authors share a famous experiment that speaks to the harm of perfectionism. They tell the story of a ceramics teacher who divided his class into two groups. One group was to focus on creating as many ceramic pieces as possible before the end of term, while the other half of the class was going to deliver one perfect piece of ceramic art in the same period. The quantity group would get an A with fifty pounds of art, and the quality group could achieve an A with one perfect piece of art.

At the end of the term, the ceramics teacher discovered that the best art came from the quantity group because they spent their time working on their craft repeatedly. The quantity group learned about technique and explored diverse methods while learning from their mistakes, becoming better artists, and improving their skills. The quality group, focused on perfection, produced one piece of inferior art. Which group would you say you fit into? Do you agonize over producing one single perfect thing, or do you move fast and learn on the go?

With marketing my work and my services on social media (which I have been doing since 2013), this message resonates. Showing up, sharing content, and sharing art is more important than creating one perfect social media post. Each time one of my posts has gone viral on various platforms, it is usually something I posted on a whim, speaking to a theme that resonates with me—and the post itself has been far from perfect. I focus on spiritual and psychological posts that offer viewers frameworks through which to heal, align, and grow, and I don't worry too much about grammar or sentence structure.

Some of us may not identify as perfectionists, and these sneaky obstacles can manifest in different ways. For example, many of my clients use makeup to direct their perfectionist tendencies. One client always brought coverup with her to parties and to school in case a blemish appeared. She would also tweeze her eyebrows religiously, making sure every hair was in place before going out in public. No surprise she was also a straight A student and a high achiever.

JOURNAL PROMPTS

Letting Go

If you knew you couldn't fail, what would you do? Where did you learn to seek perfectionism? Who taught you this behavior? Is there a deep-rooted fear behind some of your perfectionist qualities? If you're avoiding doing something you want to do, what are you afraid of? What do you want to loosen your grip on? Where does perfectionism show up in your daily life?

I've had many clients struggle with perfectionism, and it can lead to increased stress and anxiety. Being perfect all the time is an inauthentic way to live—exhausting, and, truthfully, unrealistic. For some people, perfectionism has kept them from achieving their goals because they felt that if they couldn't be perfect, why show up at all? I hope this isn't the case for you too, but if it is, we're going to talk about some tools and strategies you can use to shift this mindset and get moving again on your goals.

Perfectionism has become an avenue to protect ourselves from being seen for who we truly are at our core, instead showing the world a designed version of ourselves. It is a defense mechanism. But imagine the freedom of letting go of this perfect facade, of letting your imperfections be known. Of sharing your authentic Self with others, and making it okay for others to share their authentic selves with you, too.

Oftentimes we let the opinions of others interfere with us showing up fully. If I had to give you one piece of advice on this topic, it would be, "What other people think about me is none of my business." I encourage you to repeat this statement as you move through your day—and your life—from this point forward. Set it as an alarm on your phone. Write it on a note card. Tape it to your bathroom mirror. Create a physical label that reminds you of your new mantra. Recite it, especially when you feel that someone's opinion of you is affecting your decisions or actions. Relax into it as if you're welcoming an old friend home. It will lead to miracles.

The world needs you in your imperfection and in your most authentic state! Our species evolved from testing out diverse routes of success, and it's hard to go out into the world and make mistakes when we are trying to be perfect all the time. So how do we loosen our grip on being perfect if that's our usual state? Once you become clear that perfectionism is rooted in fear-based thoughts, your inner guru will help direct you back into alignment. Let's take a moment to move and reconnect to this guiding force.

YOGI JUMPING JACKS MEDITATION

This active meditation is one of the first practices I weave in whenever I am working with someone who is anxious, feeling stressed, or stuck in the perfectionist mentality. This practice allows you to move, open up, and follow a natural breathing pattern, bringing ease to the body. It also gives anxious energy an outlet to move through, and it will increase your heart rate and open up your shoulders and hamstrings. It is a power pose and heart-opening practice and is said to shift your mood from negative to positive—perfect for when you're stuck in a perfectionist mindset.

To start, stand with your feet wide, about hip-width-and-a-half distance apart, and stretch your arms out parallel to the floor to your side. On an inhale through your nose, expand your heart toward the sky, bending into a subtle back bend, reaching your arms back, gently opening your heart space. Then exhale through your nose, fold forward at your hips, and twist, reaching your right hand to your left foot. You can bend your knees. Inhale, stand up, and reach your arms out, gentle heart to the sky, then switch and fold forward, reaching your left hand to your right foot.

Repeat this sequence for one to three minutes, alternating sides while inhaling and exhaling through your nose. At the end of the practice, pause. Stand in stillness. How do you feel? Stand with your right hand on your heart and your left hand on your stomach. Give yourself a moment to check in and breathe.

READY IS NOT REAL

Listen. You may never feel ready. You may never feel like now is the divine time. You will never be perfect. Instead of freaking out, what needs to happen for you to relax into that?

I knew that I would never feel ready to travel the world solo; but I also knew that if I booked the plane ticket, I would show up for the flight. I knew that I would never feel ready to write a book; but I knew that if I wrote the proposal, got the agent, and secured the book deal, then writing the book was the next natural, aligned step. I would also hire the spiritual mentor, business coach, or editor and ask for help when needed. Each time I had a pie-in-the-sky goal for myself, I acted as though it were coming to fruition long before I was ready, because *I trusted I would rise to the occasion.* This feeling-state of "ready" is one of the biggest lies we tell ourselves. We think there is going to be some divine time at which everything will fall into place—and then THAT will be the time that we "do the thing we've always wanted to do." No, my love. It doesn't work like that.

Start now.
Start messy.
Start scared.
Start tired.

Start with toothpaste in the corner of your mouth and your baby's spit-up on your shirt.

Start while there is a dishwasher full of clean dishes that need to be put away.

Start today. Because today is the best day to make your dreams a reality.

One of the most important relationships you will ever have in your life is your relationship with time. Time is a human construct. It guides us human beings and forces us to operate within a twenty-four-hour structure. When I felt anxious in college or was feeling lonely during a yoga training in Kerala, I remembered that no matter what, time was moving; this moment is temporary. Time is reliable, even in our moments of unrest or discomfort. There was always going to be a holiday in which I got to be with my family in Chicago, and—eventually, even if I was living on the other side of the world—I always had some sort of return plane ticket. There was always going to be a warm cup of coffee to look forward to in the morning. I could always pick up the phone and call someone loving or cook a nostalgic meal. There were always books to explore to offer inspiration and comfort or music to calm the mind.

We can't avoid discomfort, pain, grief, loneliness, or awkwardness all the time—but when we find ourselves in a situation where we're feeling one of these heightened emotional states, we know that this too shall pass. The bad moments and the good ones, alike. So, realizing this, how is your concept of time? How do you perceive it and use it?

SOUL TIME

If we wait until we're in the mood to do "the things," we risk waiting a *looooong* time. I made time my friend. I also started the practice of Soul Time, which is my interpretation of holy "office hours." It is a scheduled chunk of time dedicated to completing your most important rituals and tasks that will get you in alignment with your dreams. Time is going to flow and go by any which way, no matter what. You cannot wait for the mood to strike before acting. Time is an ever-being, continuous element of our human experience. We can be intentional with our time or not—it's going to flow by either way.

Your great work is implementing that which you desire through aligned action. Embody the thing you most desire by setting Soul Time. I always think about Soul Time as baring my heart to God, showing up in the highest way, as if to say, "Here I am, going for it, making my dreams happen!" Do not mess around with your heart, your dreams, or these sacred moments with the Universe.

Following are a few examples of Soul Time in action along with suggested time allocations. To start, I recommend starting off with a smaller increment of time.

※ Sitting down to write for 35 minutes

※ Having a dedicated meditation practice for 18 minutes

※ Taking your children to the park to play for 22 minutes

- ❀ Going on dating apps or asking for introductions for 12 minutes

- ❀ Scheduling time to meal prep for 15 minutes

- ❀ Getting those steps in every day for 30 minutes

- ❀ Stretching your body as you wake up in the morning for 5 minutes

Listen, we are who we let ourselves be, inside and out. Remember, all the stuff that happens in your life is just stuff. We decide what circumstances influence us. We decide how we live our lives. A saying I share with my community often is, "How you spend your days is how you spend your life." It's so true. What you're doing today matters. Life occurs in the in-between, in the smaller, quieter moments. It's why Mornings with Meaning are so important, bringing that intention and breath into your life first thing every day. How we spend our mornings, afternoons, and evenings adds up—our days become our years. The radical intention-setting for what we desire our lives to be and feel like occur in the small minutes and hours of our day. For example, if you desire to be a mindful person, did you meditate today? Did you take a deep breath before you drank your cup of coffee or ate your lunch? Are you keeping up with your Mornings with Meaning?

If you desire to be a loving partner to your beloved, did you check in on them today? If you desire to be a successful entrepreneur, did you explore a new client relationship or connect with your audience via social media or email? If you desire to be an author, did you write today? If you desire to not let the bad things that occurred in the past affect you, did you come back to your breath after a negative thought? Are you making decisions rooted in your best version of Self?

So often, we have grandiose goals, not realizing that our days, and the small rituals we perform each day, lead to a life aligned with our highest dreams. Our work is to embody that version of ourselves right now. Scheduling time into your life will guide you closer to your desires, dreams, and goals. Soul Time is similar to rituals that are rooted in your daily life, and that connect you to the feeling-state you want to embody.

There is a sacred yogic proverb that says, "When the pressure is on, show up." This means that when you feel the inspiration, the urgency, or the general stress of something, take a moment, set some Soul Time, and dive in. You don't always need a lot of hours to get something done. Trust yourself that dedicating even a small amount of time can further your dreams and make an enormous difference in your life.

PROCRASTINATION

Recent research shows that procrastination is a tool we use to regulate ourselves emotionally. We procrastinate so we don't have to feel the unpleasant emotion that is paired with the thing we need to do. This is a powerful observation, because we often prioritize our feelings in the present or in the short term rather than taking care of our future Self who needs to write that paper, clean the house, get the car fixed, or "do the thing." The task we put off is living rent-free in the back of our minds, so there is always a level of awareness of it. The work here is to get clear. Why are you avoiding the thing you need to do? Notice the emotions that are associated with that thing.

I see many incredible people pause on their God-given work, the work they are meant to do in this lifetime, because they are waiting to feel inspired. This is another form of procrastination. I have seen this theme play out in my life and have found different activities that help get me into an inspired state. For example, if I have a writing deadline or need to come up with a theme to support the alignment of my clients and community, I schedule in Soul Time and take myself to a coffee shop I haven't been to before with comfy tables and chairs. I order a cappuccino and a scone. The tasty treat, the change of scenery, and the people-watching put me in an inspired state. So, don't wait to feel inspired to do the thing you've always wanted to do. Your desires and dreams are aligned with your calling in this lifetime, and the best time to pursue them is now. Be an active participant in your own life every day. Do the work you need to do to get inspired. Do the thing.

JOURNAL PROMPTS

Tackling Procrastination

What actions will you take during your Soul Time? How much time will you allocate for your Soul Time? Instead of waiting to feel compelled to act, what could you do to get into an inspired state now? How could you make the thing you need to do more fun?

BREATH OF JOY MEDITATION

This practice was introduced to me through a more feminine yogic lineage in an ashram in India, and I have also practiced this meditation in more Western yoga settings in the States. You can dive into this active meditation whenever you're feeling disconnected from yourself. (If you sit at a desk all day, this is an especially useful practice.) This is also a wonderful meditation to embody with kids. It takes a minute or less and shifts you back into a healthy headspace. Do over eleven rounds if it feels good.

To start, stand tall with your feet hip distance apart. This is a three-part inhale through your nose and one part exhale through your mouth.

Inhale through your nose and reach your hands high to the sky.

Take in a sip of air through your nose, reaching your hands out wide, parallel to the ground.

Take another sip through your nose, reaching your hands back up high to the sky.

Exhale through your mouth as you forward fold, bending your body at your hips, reaching for the earth, fingertips toward the ground. You may make a gentle "Ahh" sound with the exhale.

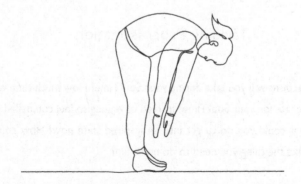

Repeat this for a minimum of eleven rounds.

At the end, sit in silent meditation or stand and take notice of how you feel. If you feel dizzy or breathless, rest and return to a natural breathing sequence.

STRETCHING TIME

I know what you're thinking: Erin, you just said time is an ever-present, non-negotiable element in our human experience! Yes, I did. But hear me out. Stretching time is when we differentiate between a disconnected, stressed-out headspace and a calm, centered, healthy headspace. Perhaps you are a business-woman, a mom, and the primary caregiver for your parents. You live a full life and your headspace is at capacity. When that "just one more thing" arises in your day, are you calm, or do you get overwhelmed? I've learned that it is more important for me to pause, take a moment to breathe, connect with my inner guru even for just a moment, and then navigate the day's chaos. This allows me to regulate my nervous system, formulate a plan, consider if there are alternatives, and then act. Hopefully, taking these few extra moments up front will mean that I'll get all my tasks done with ease the first time, from a place of alignment, rather than rushing to act only to find out that I need to backtrack or do something over again.

There is a sacred yogic proverb that says, "If you are busy, meditate for twenty minutes. If you are very busy, meditate for forty minutes." You double your devotion. You take *more* time to center as opposed to less. When you are already overwhelmed, your gut reaction is to put out the fire. That's fine, go do the thing you need to do. But once that is finished, can you pause and breathe while cutting veggies for tonight's salad, or replying to that email, or doing any other task that is not an emergency? Stretch time by pausing, breathing, and relaxing the jaw. Take a step back and connect to Self and the present moment—and then go on about your day.

TWISTER MEDITATION

This practice detoxes the internal organs, cleanses the lungs, and increases flexibility in your spine. It's a great option if you're looking for a reset after a stressful encounter, or if you're looking to pause, reconnect to Self, and come back to your breath before tackling a full day.

Begin by sitting in a comfortable posture. If you want to place a bolster, block, or pillow underneath your tailbone, do so. When you add the bolster, the goal is to rotate your pelvis forward, supporting you in realigning your spine. Try not to overexaggerate the curvature of your spine. Allow the bolster to open your hips gently.

Roll your shoulders back and place your fingertips on your shoulders, elbows bent parallel to the floor. Open your heart. There will be a ninety-degree angle between the side of your body, your armpit, and your underarm.

From this position, inhale through your nose and twist from your core to the left.

Exhale through your nose, twisting to the right.

Inhale through your nose left, exhale through your nose right. Keep this posture for one to three minutes.

Next, shift and inhale toward the right and exhale toward the left. Spend the same amount of time in this position as you did on the left. Take your time.

When you are finished, return to a neutral seated position and breathe. You can move into a silent seated meditation at this point, or you can end the exercise here and carry on with your day.

UPLEVEL MEDITATION

People ask me all the time, "Erin, what is the one thing I can do to change my life?" My answer is always the same: *Meditate.* The sooner you have a devoted, delicious, calming practice, the sooner everything in your life becomes miraculous. After living around the world and studying diverse meditations, I have found active practices to be the most transformational. This led me to creating and teaching a unique active meditation framework called UpLevel Meditation, which is geared to people with ADD, ADHD, anxiety, depression, and compulsive (sometimes negative) thought patterns. This practice focuses on intention setting, then standing active practice; then breathwork; then seated active practice and chanting. We close with a gentle, silent seated meditation. This structure has helped thousands of people get out of their own way, move closer to their goals and dreams, and deepen their connection to their inner guru.

UpLevel Meditation resonates for people who feel calmer after a run, a high-intensity interval training (HIIT) workout, or a stretchy yoga class, as it is an active practice. We need to move our bodies and open up our shoulders and hips to drop more deeply into Self. It is also beneficial for those of us who enjoy more flexible and intuitive spiritual practices.

UpLevel Meditation is not a one-size-fits-all formula. That's because it's a misconception that silent, seated meditation is the only way to meditate. In fact, because there are nearly eight billion people in this world, there are eight billion ways to meditate, eight billion ways to eat for optimum health, and eight billion ways to express soul-authenticity. You move into the active framework and trust that you will know which practices resonate with you. As with anything, you have to decide what feels in alignment and resonates with you. To understand what feels good in the body and mind, it is essential to embody and practice different styles of meditation to find your own unique code of relaxation and connection. The goal is to build your own active sequence that feels good, aiming for about eighteen minutes, just like our Mornings with Meaning. Your sequence will lead you into a calm, healthy, grounded headspace.

GUIDED INTEGRATION

That gap between where you are today and where you'd like to be a month, a year, or ten years down the road can be daunting. When your schedule is full with work, family obligations, friends, pets, personal projects, and household chores, it can be hard to figure out where there's even room to begin to make change or do the things you desire. This is where perfectionism and procrastination reign, and sometimes chaos or a life of "response" (as opposed to awareness and connection) ensues. Here are a few tools to help you reclaim your time and get moving toward the goals you have for the future.

- ☀ **Instead of being more perfect, ask, *How can I be more authentic?*** Perfectionism is one route that can prevent us from pursuing our heart's desires. Remember, it is better to produce many different things, and continuously show up, than to create one thing in the name of trying to be perfect. Try embodying yogi jumping jacks to shift your energy around perfectionism, and examine your relationship to learning through failure.

- ☀ **Remember, how you spend your days is how you spend your life.** While scheduling obligations back-to-back can soon lead to burnout, big expanses of unscheduled time can slip away, with nothing to show for them. Figure out what the right balance is for you, and make some Soul Time appointments on your calendar.

❉ **Be an active participant in your own life.** Notice when you are allowing yourself to procrastinate and push back a task that will lead you closer to your highest possible timeline. Try stretching time through the breath of joy meditation practice. And ask yourself, *What feelings am I trying to avoid by pushing back the thing I need to do?*

❉ **Meditate.** Meditation is a life-altering practice that will allow you to move throughout your life with a relaxed nervous system and a healthy headspace. UpLevel Meditation is a specific active meditation framework that allows you to move into the heightened feeling-state and work through it with breath. Take time to notice which practices resonate with you and bring them into your Morning with Meaning as a daily devotional practice.

❉ **Allow yourself to pause and regroup when plans go awry.** Rather than acting on your first thought under stress, see if you can take a beat. Do one of the meditations in this chapter to move, stretch, and recenter in your body. Twist out and realign with the grounded headspace. From there, form a new, better plan for how you'll move forward.

call god what you want, just call

We should not laugh at the person who becoming caught up in his prayer
bends his body or moves about in strange ways. Perhaps he moves in this
manner to wave off unwelcome thoughts that would interrupt the prayer.
Would we find it funny if we saw a person drowning going through strange
motions doing whatever was necessary to save his life?

—BAAL SHEM TOV

The stars were barely visible in the sky as the early morning sun prepared to make her entrance. My friend Adam was on all fours, forehead to the ground, praying to the Duomo. My roommate sat next to him, looking up at the sacred church with her hands at her heart. Devin leaned on her elbow next to Dan, who lay, on the earth, clutching a chocolate croissant. I took a bite from my kebab, put it down, and closed my eyes, leaning against the Duomo with the rest of our crew.

This morning reverence became routine for my eight-person group of study abroad friends in Florence, Italy. Between the hours of 2:00 a.m. and 4:00 a.m., we walked home from the bars and clubs, pizza or tasty snack in hand. We stopped at the Duomo, sat on the ground facing this gorgeous work of art, and paused for a moment. Half of us were Catholic, the other half were Jewish. But it didn't matter. We all sat in gratitude to the divine for allowing this to be our reality. We talked quietly with our higher power, meditated, prayed, and rested. Then the guys walked my roommates and me home before the sun rose. I loved these moments and connection through prayer.

I have been praying since the eighth grade when my maternal grandmother passed away. No one taught me how to do it; I just learned to close my eyes and talk to my Ray-Ray and to God. I have prayed every night before sleep for nearly twenty years. It's not just a habit—it's part of my life, a regular devotion to stay connected to a higher power and my ancestors. I was a spiritual child. Overly observant and curious of those around me, I wondered why bad things happen to good people. I was curious about how we all got here and would wonder about God and our intention for being here.

Sometimes you know in your core that there is a higher presence, something bigger than yourself. You know you are here for a purpose, that your work is to uncover it, align with it, and deepen it. This knowing, this feeling, is difficult to

nothing can stop you

express with language. We all have access to a higher power—should we desire to commune with it.

Your truth about God doesn't need to make sense to anyone else, yet it is also important for you to define it. I define spiritual connection as a relationship to a higher power as you understand it. Let your connection be to God, Adonai, Jesus, Allah, the Buddha, Brahma, YHWH, Mother Nature, Gaia, spirit, energy, the Universe, your ancestors, the elements, or anything else that feels aligned with you. I recommend putting a name and specific verbiage to your spiritual belief system as it defines what—or whom—you're calling on when you desire guidance.

JOURNAL PROMPTS

Exploring Your Connection with a Higher Power

What are your belief systems? Take a moment to write down your relationship to God as you understand it. If you desire to deepen your connection to God, what rituals will you do? What steps will you take?

It is essential to understand the difference between a higher power and your own inner wisdom. The distinction between your inner Self and God is that your inner guru is your intuitive internal compass, your inner teacher, your most authentic Self at your core, your gut check. Your inner guru is also parts of your personality and uniqueness, what makes you your most authentic Self. God, the

Universe, is a higher power, an ever-present energy that you can always tap into and that is always around you. The difference can also be explored as soul (your inner light) versus energy (a universal source). Soul is within. Source is bigger than Self. You may choose to connect with your inner guru and allow it to lead you to God. Or you can let these two concepts support each other and coexist.

ALIGNING YOUR INNER GURU WITH GOD ENERGY

Because I have always been close to God, on my spiritual exploration I needed to strengthen my "inner guru muscle." I wanted to explore my devotion to believing while deepening my inner guru connection. While in Israel, for example, I dedicated myself to exploring and listening to my inner guru. I led a ten-day spiritual journey throughout the whole of Israel for forty-plus North Americans and ten Israelis in early January 2015, and I planned to live there for the six months afterward to continue my soul work. This spiritual journey started off in the north hiking in the Golan Heights, then heading south to swim in the Dead Sea and climbing the sacred mountain of Masada. I would lead morning meditations, guide spiritual talks while on long bus rides, and facilitate evening programming about connecting to your morals and Jewish or spiritual identity.

After leading the ten-day experience, I arrived at my best friend Michal's apartment in Baka, Jerusalem. Michal and I had met years earlier when we'd led a teen tour through Israel, and we'd stayed close. After a few weeks of much-needed sleep (and going on dates with a guy who lived in the hills of Jerusalem who worked for the travel organization I also worked with), I realized it was time to submerse myself in a new spiritual pilgrimage. It was time to go. This was the moment I decided my next stop would be the desert ashram, a place in the middle of Negev, the Israeli desert.

It just so happened that the weekend I needed to move out of Michal's was also the weekend of a shamanic experience at the desert ashram, as I wrote about in an earlier chapter. I booked a bus ticket, packed my things, and told Michal I'd meet her in Tel Aviv in a few weeks.

On the bus on the way to the ashram, I had a freak out—just a little one. *Erin, you did it this time. Do you even know where this bus is taking you?*

"התחנה הבאה, שדה בוקר—Next stop, Sde Boker," the speaker on the bus alerted.

I sat alone at the back of the bus from Jerusalem to Sde Boker to another stop where the ashram was, wearing all my layers—a cold front was passing through the south of Israel. Mom's Gap jacket from the 1990s swaddled me and I leaned against my backpack, using it as a pillow. I chatted with some fellow travelers for a while. Just as a dust storm rolled in, the bus pulled up to the ashram.

My inner guru had guided me to this place, and some part of me knew I needed to be here. But the description of the weekend retreat was an invitation for shamans from around the world to come together, and I am not a shaman. I was in for helluva ride.

As I walked through the ashram, everyone around me started setting up tents. Oh shit. That is when I realized.

Erin, you don't have a tent!

The sun was setting.

There was dust in my mouth.

The temperature was dropping.

I was starting to shiver.

Even though I had a decades-old sleeping bag, between the cold front and the dusty desert floor, I was in a predicament. I was way outside my comfort zone. My anxiety sat on my chest like a ton of bricks. Doubt crept in. My negative thoughts mocked me for thinking I could be this free-spirited person who shows up on a whim to an ashram filled with shamans. The moment before I threw a pity party, or called Mom in tears, I practiced my true beliefs. My inner guru had guided me here for a reason. I knew it. But in that moment, I needed guidance from the Universe. I needed a presence greater than my inner guidance to redirect and support me. So, I paused. I prayed. I asked the energy around me for a miracle, a shift in perspective from fear and anxiety to inner peace. I asked for a tent. My tent. For just me. And

I vowed to pay attention.

The travelers from Sde Boker I'd met on the bus ride welcomed me into their tent. They were a few weeks away from joining the army, which is mandatory service for the majority of Israeli citizens, and, like me, they had come to the ashram to meditate, dance under the stars, and partake in the spiritual programming. At the welcoming ice-breaker session, I met another woman who invited me into her tent. But there were whispers about a midnight sex party taking place on the east side of the ashram and I was already not in the best headspace, so I knew that was not the scene for me. I laughed to myself thinking about all the sand that would end up in uncomfy places during that orgy.

I decided this was a lesson in surrender, and I put my sleeping bag in the tent with my Sde Boker friends. The temperature continued to drop. I could see my breath and was prepared to sleep in my sleeping bag to fend off the dust. Feeling defeated, I walked to the cafeteria to grab a hot tea. I stood next to a man who was about my age in line. We started chatting. We were both from Chicago! It was delightful connecting with someone from home. We even had a few mutual connections. He told me about his studies in Jerusalem and introduced me to his girlfriend, and I shared that I was on a spiritual solo exploration that had guided me here. I got my tea and was about to walk back toward my Sde Boker friends' tent when I decided, on a nudge from Spirit, to ask a particular question.

"Hey, you don't by chance have an extra tent, do you?" I asked, teeth chattering.

He took a sip of his tea. "Yeah, I do. It's small, though. It will only fit one person."

I felt the wink from God. I had a whole-body visceral reaction and even started crying a little, blaming my watery eyes on the cold weather. We walked together to his car, got the tent, and I thanked him profusely. I set up my single tent next to my Sde Boker friends and went from feeling anxious to feeling grounded in my body and my spiritual connection.

The magic kept happening. I met a shaman who knew everything about me. I witnessed a spiritual exorcism that blew my mind. I danced and meditated in the desert sun, solo hiked the desert, and connected with people from all around Europe and the Middle East. There were rumors that Moses received the ten commandments here. The ashram in the desert demanded growth, trust, and surrender, and the entire experience was a powerful lesson on the alignment that happens between one's inner guru connection and God unity.

EMBODIMENT PRACTICE:
PAUSE, PRAY, PAY ATTENTION

You may have done this practice before without even knowing it. This is a method of prayer you can use when you feel the intensity of a moment leading you into a negative feeling-state. This is a prayer you can use when you feel like hitting your knees, giving up, and making friends with rock bottom. Whenever you're in a pressure-cooker situation and emotions are high, use this framework. If you can remind yourself to take a deep breath and implement this practice, you will be redirected.

Step 1: Pause. When you feel into an intense moment, pause whatever you are doing. Move into a prostration pose (allow yourself to stretch and face toward the earth, similar to child's pose in yoga), or move to sitting on your knees with your head tilted forward in a bow. Choose a pose that feels like surrender in your body. Take a deep breath. Sometimes I will chant "Om" three times, wash my hands, change my socks, or light a beeswax candle to differentiate this moment from all others. It is important that your pause is intentional to mark a shift in time.

Step 2: Pray. Connect to a higher power as you understand it. Ask for what you need to feel better. This is not a time to "pray away" a bad feeling-state, but a mindful moment to come back to the present. This is a time for you to notice how you feel and to ask for a redirection. Be clear on what it is you need. You can ask for a specific thing that may help you feel safer or ask for a feeling-state of peace, clarity, alignment, or ease.

For example, perhaps you will ask to meet someone from your hometown, as you know this will make you feel safe. You could also ask to see a specific symbol that is important to you that will show you that you are protected. I always work with deer and ask to see deer, as they remind me of where I grew up in Chicago. I will say, "God, show me deer so I know I am on the right path." (When Jon proposed to me on the scenic beach in our hometown, four deer came out of the woods to witness the proposal. Another powerful sign!)

Step 3: Pay attention. Once you've paused and prayed, pay attention to the shift. If someone calls you out of the blue, pick up the phone. If someone slides in your DMs asking for support, accommodate them if it feels right to. When you ask for a symbol, make sure that you're awake enough to see it when it comes. Be an active participant in your own life by staying alert for redirection.

Try this practice in moments that feel extreme and in moments in which you want a shift in perspective. This practice is also a self-awareness technique, whereby you can pinpoint the beginning of an emotion and redirect it before it becomes a full-blown panic attack. Your job is to remember this method in the heat of the moment.

EMBODIMENT PRACTICE: HITBODEDUT הִתְבּוֹדְדוּת -

In Judaism there is a spiritual practice called *hitbodedut* wherein you take time to talk out loud to God in unstructured prayer. If you are new to prayer (or if it feels foreign to you), and yet you desire to deepen your spiritual connection, try this practice. I use the term God here to reference the divine, but insert whatever higher power verbiage resonates with you.

To start, go for a walk in nature or someplace you feel safe and connected. Set the intention that you are on this walk not just to enjoy the walk, but to practice this sacred ritual.

Start talking to God in a way that feels comfortable to you. Speak from your heart. Release the need to have a beginning, middle, or end to the dialogue. Just speak your thoughts aloud. Talk for as long or as short a time as you desire.

When I learned this practice, I asked the rabbi, "Why out loud? If it's just me and God, can't I just speak in my mind?" The rabbi shared that when you speak out loud, you are less likely to get distracted and more likely to be present and holy with your words. When we dialogue with ourselves internally, sometimes we skip words or shift from one topic to the next or lose focus and fall asleep (if laying down). Speaking out loud keeps us present in the practice, and we use more of our senses, like hearing and speaking, to witness our experience.

Try your best to be holy with your words. Speak with precision, avoid filler words when possible, and share from a place of truth and authenticity. Assume that God knows who you are at your core, so there is no need to catch God up on what has been going on in your life. Just dive right in.

When you've come to a stopping point, close the practice with gratitude. Say "thank you" to yourself for showing up and to God for being your witness.

Before returning to the natural rhythm of your day, pause. Listen. Sometimes there will be a response. Be open to receiving. Take a couple deep breaths or place your hands on the earth to bring you back to a grounded headspace.

Try this out once a week or do it when you feel inspired. How does the ritual feel in your body? Over time, you will deepen your relationship with God. Remember, your work is to pay attention. The topics you discuss with God may reach a new level of understanding, or perhaps you will work out an obstacle in your life with ease. Notice the small shifts that lead to big changes over time.

JOURNAL PROMPTS

Reflecting on Your Conversations with God

What is an obstacle you're moving through that God may be able to help with? Where can you walk outside and speak aloud with no one overhearing? What insights have you gained after talking with God?

NURTURING A SPIRITUAL CHILD

My mentor professor at Columbia University, Dr. Lisa Miller, is the author of the bestselling book *The Spiritual Child.* In her research-backed book, Miller illustrates how important it is for the well-being of children to have a strong spiritual connection, and she shares case studies and stories of how such children experience less depression and are also less likely to abuse drugs.

Parents are responsible for nurturing their children and helping them cultivate their spiritual connection. Miller clarifies that spiritual development is not defined as prayer in the school systems or mainstream religion. Instead, it is encouraging children to be curious and explorative through a more universally understood spiritual lens. For example, having the ability to communicate with animals, having compassion for people years younger or older than them, or having the capacity to foster a connection to something bigger than Self are all the makings of a spiritual child.

Children come into this world connected to spirit in their own unique way. I recommend reading the book *The Little Soul and the Sun* by Neale Donald Walsch, a beautiful story that explains difficult-to-understand spiritual themes to children (and adults, too!).

Here are some ideas on nurturing spirituality with children:

※ Invite them to get curious.

※ Ask them questions about why they made a spiritually minded decision.

※ Take them into nature. Observe how they communicate with plants, trees, soil, and the landscape.

※ When they meet animals like dogs and cats, ask them how they feel in the company of these animals.

※ Welcome hard questions. We, as adults, don't need to have all the answers. Saying, "I'm not sure. What do you think?" when a child asks a question is a wonderful place to start.

※ Show them a sunset and ask them what they see.

※ Ask them if they remember their dreams, or where they were before they were earthside, or if they think they chose their parents.

※ Play music with them.

※ Offer them a blank piece of paper and colorful crayons. Invite them to explore using the colors and a blank canvas.

- ❋ When a child stares off into the distance, ask them what they see, or what they are thinking.

- ❋ Be as patient as possible with big emotions from children. They are learning about themselves and the world at a rapid pace.

Nurturing a spiritual child is going to look different for every family. The biggest takeaway is to encourage children to be curious safely. If organized religion is part of your family's customs, invite the child to add their own flavor to the ritual.

GUIDED INTEGRATION

Our inner guru is our internal compass, and God is an ever-present energy bigger than Self. These two themes work together to deepen your spiritual connection and support you in living aligned to your highest possible timeline. Take time to contemplate your connection to their symbiotic relationship.

- ❋ Get on a first name basis with your higher power. Pick a specific verbiage that feels holy to you and name what you refer to as a higher power as you understand it. Take time daily to connect with this bigger-than-Self energy.

- ❋ The PPP method will guide you back to yourself. The next time you feel a heightened emotional state and out of alignment, pause, pray, and pay attention. This method is a powerful surrender and prayer practice that will offer you guidance, unique clarity, and course correction.

❋ Practice Hitbodedut. Go on a walk in nature and speak unedited to this higher power as you understand it to deepen your connection. You can also use this practice to ask questions and gain clarity on a choice or situation you desire guidance on.

❋ Spiritually nurture children. Whether you are a parent or not, notice opportunities where you can encourage the children in your life to exercise their natural curiosity and connection to animals, nature, and other people.

CHAPTER 9

give yourself an experience, not an explanation

Trust yourself. Create the kind of self that you will be happy to live with all your life. Make the most of yourself by fanning the tiny, inner sparks of possibility into flames of achievement.

—GOLDA MEIR

Listen, love, sit down. Breathe. Real talk. One day, you will expire. Your soul will leave your human "meat suit." You will die. This life is transitory, and, as they say, no one gets out of here alive. If you had a chance to look back and ask yourself a few questions, what would your answers be? Were you spending your time doing what made you happy? Did you chart a course that reflected what you really valued? Did you go on incredible trips? Make out with interesting people? Eat delicious foods? No? Were you too busy worrying about what other people thought of you? Were you working hard to afford your lifestyle, only to realize that some of what you were doing was making you sad, disconnected, or unhealthy? Were you too busy to take a second and sit with your own thoughts because you feared what would come up?

I don't want to label this as "tough love" because it is just love. It is truth. Confronting your mortality is a sacred spiritual practice. Sitting back, enjoying an easy ride, or staying passive isn't cute—and, for sure, it's not interesting. Are you playing small? Maybe you realize it during a yoga class when your mind wanders off to all the creative entrepreneurial ideas that live scattered in your head. Or you scroll through others' travel photos online and a jolt of envy slices through you. Perhaps you stare at yourself in the mirror and notice that even though you look the same, so much has shifted beneath the surface. Breathe in. This is your time to seize the day, your moment to show up.

LEGACY ENERGY AND YOU

So often we move throughout our lives questioning our purpose or our mission for why we are here, on earth, in this moment in time. Legacy energy is focusing on the feeling-state we want to leave the world with after we expire. It is the mark we offer the world and its people day in and day out until the moment of expiration.

As we dive into this next chapter together, we'll consider an interesting school of psychology called existential psychotherapy. Existential psychotherapy is encompassed by the phrase "The patient doesn't need an explanation; they need an experience." This school of psychology focuses on meaning and an awareness that everyone's life span has an end date. I find existential psychotherapy techniques, such as joining a live event or retreat, lead to massive growth because you embody transformation—feel it deep within—and then can heal, align, and grow from there. Because once you have the experience, the feeling of knowing how good it can get, you have a better idea of how to stay connected as you move forward.

Existential psychotherapy offers you an opportunity to make a real-time shift or adopt an alternative perspective. Your expiration is guaranteed—it's just a matter of when. I don't say this to make you uneasy. I bring it up because it is a reframe-and-refocus tool to align you with what matters in this lifetime. This is the truth. When you reverse engineer from the truth, you can realign with what you want to be known for and with the legacy you will leave behind.

Once you know what you want your legacy to be, you can shine that legacy energy out into the world. Legacy energy is the long-lasting impact you leave the world with once you depart. So often I work with clients who are focusing on scaling their businesses to seven figures or climbing the corporate ladder. Some clients move throughout their days as busy parents on autopilot. They practice this legacy energy work and realize, "*Oh.* Oh, wow. This is not in alignment with how I want to be remembered—by my loved ones, or by myself." When you do this exercise, some parts of your legacy energy will resonate, but in other parts, you might need course correction.

EMBODIMENT EXERCISE:
THE DEPARTURE MESSAGE

Take a moment to connect with your breath. Inhale for a count of five. Hold the inhale at the top for a count of six and exhale for a count of seven. Practice this nervous-system-relaxing meditation for one to three minutes, or until you feel calm within. Invite in a beginner's mind; there is no right or wrong way to connect to this practice.

Once you feel grounded and connected to your body, picture golden, braided roots extending downward from the base of your tailbone, moving through the floor, into the earth, and connecting to earth's core. You're grounded, you're centered, you're present. Breathe in. Visualize the golden, braided roots.

See yourself standing on a small stage. You walk toward the podium. Slowly, you feel the wooden podium under your hands as you stand tall, facing the audience. You look out into the crowd—you see people you have met over your lifetime, friends, family, coworkers, people you love, and people who love you.

You look down at the podium and see a stack of paper. The title on the top page says "My Eulogy." You take a moment to recenter yourself. You are at your own funeral, reading your eulogy. Be gentle, love. This specific eulogy dives into all areas of your life, milestones that matter to you, and how people felt in your presence. Take a deep breath. Write your eulogy in your journal.

Once you have finished writing, come back to your breath. How do you feel? What themes came up for you? This is a powerful moment for reflection. Picture the golden, braided roots at the base of your tailbone. Relax the muscles in your face and release your tongue from the roof of your mouth. Swallow. Unclench your stomach, relax your pelvic floor, wiggle your toes. Come back to your physical body. Notice the surrounding smells, the taste in your mouth, this book in your hand.

Write down five feeling-states that came up for you during the eulogy practice. How do you desire others to remember you? For example, maybe these
feeling-states are important to you:

She made everybody feel like a somebody.
To know her was to love her.
She was always just a phone call away and always made me feel better.
*She was an expander in my life, and she inspired everyone to pursue their
dreams.*
She danced to the beat of her own heart.

Write down five feeling-states that came up for you during the eulogy practice for how you desire to remember yourself. For example, maybe you resonate
with these feeling-states:

I took time to understand a skill or complete a complex project.
I showed up for my deepest desires and dreams.
I did the best I could given what I knew.
*I am proud of how I parented, loved my partner, and loved myself. I found
joy in the small moments.*
I was gentle on myself.

When looking at the feeling-states you wrote above, ask yourself, "Is this in
alignment to how I show up most days in my life?" Legacy energy means you
are showing up, as often as possible, in alignment with how you desire to be
remembered.

JOURNAL PROMPTS

Honoring Legacy Energy

What are five things you're doing today that are in alignment with how you want others to remember you? What are five things you could add into your everyday life (these could be small rituals) to be in alignment with how you want others to remember you?

BECOMING THE BENEFICIAL PRESENCE

How do you feel in your own company? What do you love about yourself? What activities do you like to do solo?

What would have to happen for you to foster a deeper connection with yourself?

When you foster a relationship with yourself, you can show up for those around you in a bigger way. You can become what Dr. Thomas Hora, the founder of Metapsychiatry, called the "beneficial presence." Hora believed that modern-day, conventional psychiatric practices did not always lead to healing, so he pursued a more wholesome, spiritual route. Dr. Hora was a physician of the soul. "All problems are psychological, and all solutions are spiritual," he said. He brought spirituality, not religion, to his patients to support them on their healing path.

I learned of Hora's work through one of my favorite professors at Columbia, who signed off his emails with "PAGL," an acronym for Peace, Assurance, Gratitude, and Love. This phrase reminds us that when we speak and live from a place of PAGL, we are connected to spirituality and the harmonic whole. Dr. Hora wanted PAGL to be another term for the connection to and awareness of God—something bigger than oneself. You can think of PAGL as a law you can use to discern whether your thoughts, beliefs, and actions are in alignment, and if you're moving in the best direction for your life.

Dr. Hora's teachings embody the beneficial presence, and they affected me deeply. My interpretation of the beneficial presence is the person in any room or circumstance who offers a safe space, who listens, or who offers kind energy. Dr. Hora believed that to live aligned with PAGL, you show up as the compassionate beneficial presence. When I started studying Dr. Hora's teachings, I set my phone alarm to go off a couple times during the day saying, "beneficial presence," a reminder to me to show up as my most compassionate Self. I just looked at my phone now—the alarm is still there!

JOURNAL PROMPTS

Practicing PAGL and Being a Beneficial Presence

Do you live a life connected to peace, assurance, gratitude, and love? Who is the beneficial presence in your life? When are you the BP for others?

THE LAW OF MASSIVE ALIGNED ACTION

Buckle up—everything you desire is on the other side of the law of massive aligned action (LMAA). We've hinted at taking aligned action in earlier chapters, but this is where we'll really dive in to this important concept. The law of massive aligned action means you take radical, real-time action on your deepest desires and dreams today. For example, if you want to be remembered as a wonderful sister, when was the last time you called your sibling? If you want to be remembered as an inspirational coach or teacher, when was the last time you posted a unique thought on social media? If you desire to be remembered as an engaged and loving parent, how often do you put away your phone or computer when you're with your children?

Alignment will feel different for every single person. It is when your thoughts, values, morals, and beliefs are all in harmony. I like to explain alignment by exploring the feeling of hanging out with my good friends versus the feeling I get before hanging out with people who are not my cup of tea. That is one way to feel the difference.

For this law to be most effective, it is important to honor your pitfalls. Be honest with yourself. For example, do you pull back before finishing a project or fail to complete it? Do you feel as though you have shown up for yourself in the biggest way possible? Do you self-sabotage? If so, accountability will be an important factor for you to consider. Write down some shortcomings in your journal.

Can you decide for yourself right now? This means deciding that today is the day you make the needed decision to move forward on your desires and dreams. Once you decide you are going to pursue the thing you have always wanted, the magic unfolds.

In your journal, write, "I am ready. Show me how good it can get."

Then answer this question: "What do I need to do to make my legacy energy a reality?"

Reread your eulogy exercise. How do you want people to remember you? Write your wishes in an "I am" statement format in your journal. For example, if your legacy energy is all about other people feeling calm in your presence, your statement could be,

"I am calm, centered, and present."

THE LAW OF MASSIVE ALIGNED ACTION FRAMEWORK

There are four main steps to activating the law of massive aligned action: reading your "I am" statements first thing in the morning, scheduling Soul Time, resetting with the PPP method, and recalling your "I am" statements before you go to sleep. Let's look at each one.

Step 1: Upon rising, read your "I am" statements. This gets you into the energy of who you want to be throughout your day. I have my statements on my bathroom mirror, and I read them while brushing my teeth. I recommend making them a screensaver background on your phone too.

Step 2: Plan and schedule in your Soul Time. Remember, we all came into this earth in physical form so we need to take physical action. Soul Time is your nonnegotiable amount of time where you show up and "do the thing" that will get you closer to your desire.

Step 3: Practice the PPP method. Throughout the day, pay attention to when you're aligned with your legacy energy and when you drift away from it. If you notice yourself shifting into some headspace or activity that is out of alignment, take a breath. Connect with your inner guru and use the PPP method. Pause. Pray. Use the mantra, "I recognize I am out of alignment, and I choose to realign," and then Pay Attention to what feels like a realignment or a shift back into legacy energy.

Step 4: As you drift to sleep, recite your "I am" statements from memory as best you can, so they can seep into your subconscious mind and your dream state. Visualize yourself embodying the feeling-state of your legacy energy. Chant them to Self. Feel the words in your body. For example, if your "I am" statement is "I am mindful," picture yourself participating in mindful rituals and activities.

When we wake up in the morning and as we drift off to sleep we are in a theta brain wave state, which allows your mind to be more open to suggestion. This is the gateway to the subconscious mind, where our deep programmed beliefs lie. You are reprogramming your subconscious beliefs with the "I am" statements, taking physical action during the day with soul time, and realigning when needed with the PPP method. Adding in the law of massive aligned action will guide you to your dreams.

One of my favorite routes to internalize my mantras is something I learned at summer camp. I grew up going to an all-girls sports camp in Wisconsin on a quaint Midwestern lake. My cabin mates, many of whom are still my closest friends today, and I would spend the days swimming in the cool water, going on jogs toward the all-boys camp (in hopes of catching a glimpse!), and competing in capture the flag. Every year, there was a big competition called "The Sing." The goal was to create a song with unique lyrics related to that year's theme using a well-known song as the melody structure, and whichever song was best, won! I love making up lyrics for songs. So, what I do now is sing my "I am" statements to myself all day long. The tune shifts. Right now the tune is "Popular" from the musical *Wicked*. The song presses the message deeper into my being and I hum along through daily life.

THE LIMINAL ACTION

With legacy energy and this eulogy practice, you may notice this theme: the magic happens in the in-between. Think about what your in-between moments are, and what's important and transformational about them in your life—those are your liminal action moments. The liminal action is the thing that happens, almost as a side effect, that seems so small, but when reflecting on our relationships in our lives, they are the big moments.

One day, my mom and I were reflecting on the relationships in our lives and talking about the people who made it to our bigger life events—weddings, birthdays, family functions, etc. What I learned from the power of liminal action is that while it's nice when people attend your milestones, the true magic in a relationship occurs in those in-between moments: the afternoon check-in phone call, the meeting for a quick love walk, a parent waking up early with their child, or the "just thinking of you" pop-in. Life occurs in the in-between.

Whenever I am with Mom, we have a morning cup of coffee and we cry. We call it a coffee-and-cry. It's our unique ritual where we tell stories, laugh, reflect, and check in, and it usually leads to happy tears. My sister, Danielle, calls me every day when she walks home from work. I always pick up, even if I only have a minute to connect. I mark time every Friday around sunset for Shabbat, the Jewish day of rest, by lighting candles or having a glass of natural wine. Every night when Jon walks through the door, I gush at him and hold out my arms until he comes over and kisses me. These are the smaller, liminal action moments that add up and align me with my legacy energy. It isn't about the big holiday events—although, of course, I still appreciate those. It's the smaller moments in between the big ones that make up our lives. Because, as I said earlier, how we spend our days is how we spend our lives.

JOURNAL PROMPT

Appreciating Liminal Actions

What liminal actions in your life are aligned with your legacy energy?

GUIDED INTEGRATION

In this chapter, we get clear and bridge the gap between how you'd like to be perceived by others and how/if your daily actions support that goal. We remember our mortality and reverse engineer what a life of alignment looks like for us.

❀ Ask yourself, what will my legacy be? What feeling-states do you desire other people to experience when they spend time with you?

This is also a moment to face your dreams and decide how you truly want to be remembered.

✳ Remember that you are temporary. Confronting your mortality can be an intense experience. However, it is important when working with legacy energy. You can work with the eulogy exercise if you are feeling out of alignment—this will reconnect you to what really matters in this life and your legacy energy.

✳ Be the BP. The beneficial presence is one way to connect with your best version of Self. This allows you to live a life connected to compassion.

✳ Make your dreams a reality with LMAA. The law of massive aligned action is a powerful framework that will guide you toward the life you want to live through a step-by-step process.

✳ Don't forget the liminal spaces. That half hour after work when you catch up with your kids or your partner, the Sunday morning coffee with a friend, the five-minute check-in with your aunt on your commute—those small moments can matter as much or more than the big life milestones.

CHAPTER 10

what stories are you telling yourself?

Remember, you have been criticizing yourself for years, and it hasn't worked.
Try approving of yourself and see what happens.

—LOUISE HAY, YOU CAN HEAL YOUR LIFE

"I'm getting old. I can't believe I'm about to celebrate another birthday," a woman said to me at a barbecue while holding her five-year-old daughter. "I am so, so old. I just *hate* aging," she whined. I made an excuse about needing to help my friend and slipped away from the conversation. I didn't know this woman, and it's not uncommon for people to share their woes with me, but I didn't like how she was speaking about aging in general—especially in front of her daughter. This did not set a good example for all the women younger than the complainer.

Aging is just a number that keeps track of time. I have met people in their late eighties living life with more gusto than people in their thirties. I have met women in their early twenties who had the wisdom of great-grandmothers. Age is relative. It is an experience. It does not define you. And it is essential for women to reclaim the aging process as society portrays it as a negative societal construct. It is a true gift to add more candles to our birthday cakes.

"I am" is a phrase we throw around in our day-to-day life, not realizing how holy those words are. One of the first things I say to anyone new to my community is, "If you desire to heal, align, and grow, watch your tongue." What you say about yourself matters. Your inner dialogue is sacred. Your body is always eavesdropping on the thoughts circulating in your mind. Want to change your life?

Pay attention to the words you speak.

When you say "I am" and then you say something negative, you are talking shit about the most important person in your life. As you move through your day, pay attention to when you use the words "I am." Notice what you say after them. Is it positive or negative? Becoming aware is the first step in speaking kindly to yourself.

The other day, I was catching up with one of my friends on the phone. She'd made a simple mistake at work and said, "Ugh! I'm such an idiot!" I cut her off. "Don't talk about my friend like that," I said. It stopped her in her tracks. She took a moment and collected herself. It was a powerful moment of reflection.

If you would never allow someone to speak unkindly about your best friend, your sister, or any other loved one, why are you nonchalant when you speak poorly about yourself? You are a living, breathing being, a child to someone; you are both the highlight and heroine in someone else's story. You are the inspiration for a stranger who never knew your name and you must treat yourself with care. Reground. Shift your language. When you notice yourself using unkind inner dialogue, say, "Don't talk about my friend like that!"

In Dr. Wayne Dyer's book *Wishes Fulfilled,* he talks about using "I am" statements as you drift off to sleep to reprogram the subconscious mind. The subconscious mind is best known for deciding things without a thought, moving on autopilot and without needing to contemplate anything. Your conscious mind, on the other hand, is aware of the temperature in the room, the sounds nearby, and the taste in your mouth right now. The subconscious mind runs in the background without your attention. So, keep your subconscious mind on your team by filling it with positive thoughts and intentions. You can do this in your Mornings with Meaning, during meditation, by working with the law of massive aligned action, or just before you fall asleep.

The time before you fall asleep and those early moments upon waking up are sacred. You are more open to suggestion. I recommend choosing wisely how you spend your time during these vulnerable moments in your day. In Chapter 9, I wrote about the law of massive aligned action and weaving in "I am" statements early in the morning and in those moments before falling asleep. Letting intentional "I am" thoughts seep into your subconscious is a powerful manifestation tool and an effective way of reprogramming your mind.

When you use the phrase "I am" and follow it with something negative, you are communicating with yourself and your subconscious mind. We know that what you focus on grows, so if you make fun of yourself, use your life as the butt of a joke, or self-deprecate, that feeling-state can expand. It is essential that you edit your inner and outer dialogue and foster a loving relationship with yourself.

JOURNAL PROMPTS

Examining Your Inner Dialogue

Write or refine your "I am" statements here. If you speak poorly about yourself, what mantra can you use to redirect you toward positive inner dialogue? What activities do you want to do in the morning and before bed, when you are most open to suggestion?

EMBODIMENT PRACTICE: RECORD YOUR OWN "I AM" STATEMENTS

Playing back recordings of your own voice is a great way to deepen your relationship with yourself and increase your self-admiration. Do you reach for your phone upon rising in the morning to read the news, watch a show, or scroll on social media? If so, your phone could be a powerful tool for self-growth. There are two ways to work with this practice using your phone.

To start, take out your phone and go to the voice memo or voice recording app.

Option 1: Click record on your voice memo app and recite all your "I am" statements in your own voice. Make sure you are saying each "I am" statement at least three times.

Option 2: Click record on your voice memo app, and as you embody your "I am" statements, talk about what your life looks like as if you are already living on your highest possible timeline. Record for three to five minutes, diving into the details of your day. Use phrases like "I am," "I feel," "I move," or "I act."

Around the same time every day, listen to your recording. Instead of scrolling on your phone in the morning, lie on your back, breathe, and listen to your recording. You can even play the recording while you shower or brush your teeth. It's another wonderful tool to help you communicate with your subconscious mind—using your own voice. With regular practice, your recording app can help you make your dreams a reality.

POSITIVE AFFIRMATION MEDITATION

Whether you are working on manifesting or reprogramming your subconscious mind, this is a powerful practice. You can also use this meditation if you notice yourself spiraling into negative thought patterns or you are having negative feelings about yourself.

First, create three to six different "I am" statements to call in what you most desire. For example,

1. I am in a committed, loving relationship.

2. I am healthy, whole, and healed.

3. I am a peaceful mother.

4. I am a kind voice in my own head.

5. I am supported by my team.

6. I am an inspiring teacher.

Put some beautiful music on in the background. Relax your body. For this meditation, you can be in any posture. You can lie down and drift off to sleep or sit comfortably and hold an intention.

Inhale and exhale a few times. Clear and ground yourself. Inhale through your nose and notice your lower belly expand. Exhale through your mouth with a sigh. Repeat for two or three rounds. Once you arrive in your body, inhale. Chant "I am." Exhale while stating your "I am" statements. Continue this practice for three to five minutes.

You are always welcome to switch how this meditation is chanted. I will sometimes follow this pattern:

Minute one: Chant out loud.

Minute two: Chant in a quiet whisper.

Minute three: Chant in your own inner voice, silently.

Minute four: Whistle (or some version of a whistle—no need to be a pro!).

Minute five: Chant out loud.

When practicing this with a group, it is empowering to hear your own affirmations and those of your fellow meditators. This is another great tool to help you witness your growth.

WATCH YOUR TONGUE

When pursuing your highest possible timeline and becoming aware of how you speak, you may notice some common terms that feel negative. The English language has phrases that support limiting beliefs, and we say these phrases all the time, normalizing negative collective thinking.

Here are a few examples:

* ✳ "Oh, such is life!" I noticed myself saying this phrase when I was doing something fun and it eventually had to come to an end. As if to say, as all things good come to an end. At my core I do not believe this and know that good things can keep continuing. You can try substituting this phrase with the manta, "This, or something better."

* ✳ "It's always something!" Jon and I recently got back from this great trip, and in the thick of the summer heat we hopped in our car to grocery shop. Immediately we noticed the air-conditioning wasn't working and Jon said, "Ugh, it's always something!" As if there can never be consistent peace and something aggravating always must be going on. We also use this phrase when it comes to specific people—"It's always something with him!"—as if they are the person always causing or enticing drama. If you use this phrase in reference to someone, you will that sentiment into being; there will, in fact, always seem to be something with them. Try to reframe this idea with a phrase like "and the plot thickens" or "the adventure continues!" to keep energy positive and lifted.

* ✳ "It is what it is." Now this one drives me bananas. This phrase is used as a discussion-ender, as if you have no power over a situation. It feels

like a slap in the face. We say this often when we feel we can't change an outcome or we are helpless. With the art of possibility we know there are many possible options and routes that can happen at every given time, so try to reframe with that knowing.

☀ "Just waiting for the other shoe to drop." When something bad happens, it's as if we have normalized more bad things that can happen. Instead, try shifting the energy to focus on inviting more positive and fun engagements into your life.

Here are a few other tips that I'd like to share on this topic that are more than just phrases: Try to not sing negative song lyrics about Self. I remember dancing in my friend's room in fifth grade and singing Pink's new song "Don't Let Me Get Me," which is a string of negative words using "I am" statements about how hazardous we are to ourselves. Songs are a slippery slope because they oftentimes get stuck in our heads. We do not want to speak poorly about Self even through a song. Note: The opposite is also true. There are many beautiful, uplifting spiritual songs with positive lyrics that would be incredible to get stuck into your head!

Another big recommendation is to try not to watch scary movies. Our emotional brain does not always understand that something is happening on the screen and not happening to you personally. Scary movies can leave you feeling on edge, taking you away from nourishing feeling-states. These are all suggestions—and, as always, I suggest that you edit according to what reso- nates with you.

REFRAME AND REFOCUS

In the world of positive psychology, there is a technique referred to as "positive reframing," which you can use to shift the direction of an event, situation, or conversation toward the positive. For example, if you think about something that occurred in the past that felt negative, positive reframing encourages you to observe what lessons you may have learned from that event. Could there have been a silver lining?

. . . .

Note: *This technique is not always appropriate for certain situations. I'm not suggesting that you try to find a silver lining in a tragic accident, for example. But for moments of conflict and reflection, reframing things can and will help.*

. . . .

A strategy I like to use with my clients, Reframe and Refocus, differs from positive reframing, but it has a similar goal: it incorporates a zoom-out method.

Visualize two people standing on a sidewalk. Person number one, standing on one side of the sidewalk, sees the number six written in chalk on the cement. Person number two, standing on the opposite side, says, "Are you bananas? That's the number nine." When you zoom out, both people are right. When you reframe things, shift your perspective, and observe a situation from a new vantage point, you can understand things differently.

For example, when a client is stuck in comparison, or is judging another person, I ask them to reframe and refocus. You never know if all the stories you are telling yourself in any given moment are true. You can only speculate because you have not experienced the obstacles or pleasures of that other person's life. Whether you are comparing or judging, you are doing it in a moment in time.

Do your best to mind your own thoughts. Everybody you see has diverse challenges that they don't broadcast to the world.

Facing a hard decision? Try the Reframe and Refocus method.

Zoom out.

JOURNAL PROMPT

Reframing a Situation

Who are you without your story? We bring so much of our history into our decision-making. When we release our story and zoom out, we can choose our highest possible timeline without a fear-based back story.

Reframe and Refocus reminds you that you are a temporary human being. You are having a spiritual experience on a planet called Earth. Earth is floating through a vast universe filled with many planets and galaxies. This modality offers you a perspective to guide you on what matters to you in this lifetime—that's what it looks like to align with your legacy energy.

Try saying any of these phrases out loud when you face an inexplicable obstacle and you are working on positive reframing:

"And that's rock and roll, baby!"

"It's just another chapter in my next bestseller!"

"And that is why you always pack extra underwear."

"This door closing doesn't feel good now, but it leads to an open window."

THE RULE OF THREES

One of my graduate school professors shared an uplifting and inspiring concept during class one day about listening to our intuition. Let's say, for example, that you are at lunch with some girlfriends. Out of nowhere, you have a thought. Perhaps the thought is related to the topic being discussed, or perhaps it is random. You don't want to interrupt the conversation, so you allow the thought to drift away.

The lunch continues. Again, the thought pops back in your head. And you think, *Well this is odd, why does this random thought keep coming up?* Still, you ignore it.

The check arrives. As you reach into your purse to pay, the thought comes again. This is the third time this random thought has come through. The Rule of Threes guides you to share your thoughts with your friends. When you share the thought, one of your girlfriends gets excited because that idea was the exact thing she needed to hear to feel better about an obstacle in her life.

The Rule of Threes is a tool you can use to strengthen your intuitive messages. When my professor shared this practice with the class, I implemented it right away in my personal and professional life. The Rule of Threes has led to some miraculous unfoldings, including my best friend Caroline landing a new job opportunity, me calling a friend who was in a dark depression and needed to hear an uplifting voice, and supporting my clients through much-needed breakthroughs. Pay attention if you continuously receive the same message three times.

GUIDED INTEGRATION

We've all had to contend with self-judgment and self-limiting beliefs at times. For some of us, though, these negative thoughts can become cyclical, and they're self-fulfilling prophecies. In this chapter, we learn a few tools to help stop the cycle and encourage positive "I am" statements that will build us up and help keep us on the path aligned to our goals.

- ✹ **Watch your tongue.** What you speak about Self matters. This is one way we communicate to our subconscious mind and we want to nurture healthy and positive thoughts about ourselves.

- ✹ **Work with "I am" statements.** "I am" statements are powerful and will help you embody that which you most desire. Use a recording of yourself or the "I am" meditation practice to deepen your connection to these positive statements.

- ✹ **Create a mantra you can come back to when you want to redirect your thoughts.** If you notice a negative thought-spiral about Self, find a mantra to bring you back to a loving headspace. Here's one you can work with: "Don't talk about my friend or loved one like that!"

- ✹ **If you notice you're judging yourself or others, zoom out.** Reframing the situation will allow you to think more clearly, become more open to other possibilities, and see things from a different perspective.

- ☀ **Learn to distinguish between random thoughts and your intuition.** If a thought keeps popping up repeatedly, maybe it's worth following up on by working with the rule of threes.

finding nourishment inside and out

*Compulsive eating is basically a refusal to be fully alive.
No matter what we weigh, those of us who are compulsive eaters have
anorexia of the soul. We refuse to take in what sustains us.
We live lives of deprivation. And when we can't stand it any longer, we binge.
The way we are able to accomplish all of this is by the simple act of bolting–
of leaving ourselves–hundreds of times a day.*

—GENEEN ROTH, WOMEN FOOD AND GOD

Melissa sat in the chair and wept. She brought her hands to her face and covered her eyes. She sighed. Sniffled. As the fluorescent lights shone down on her, I stared at my boss, Flora, who sat on the other side of the room, nonreactive, observing. I grabbed a tissue box from the desk and placed it next to Melissa. During this time I was Flora's mentee, training under her to become a health consultant at her health coaching practice.

"It's just..." Melissa cried through her hands. "I've got a family event coming up, a business luncheon, and I'm just not sure I can do it. It's too much change."

I sat there, a quiet witness, as Melissa worked through her emotions. I could see how desperately she wanted to change and create a new life for herself, how she was struggling to overcome and outgrow her obstacles. And, in that same space, I observed that she was also attached to them. She felt safe in them.

"I don't know if I can maintain this new diet and lifestyle with so many stressful events coming up," Melissa said with conviction. And that's what this nutrition counseling session was all about. It wasn't about food prep. She had everything sorted. It wasn't about the meal plan directions; everything was written out. It wasn't a lack of information. She had resources, including what to buy from the grocery store to reach the wellness goals she'd set for herself when she'd paid in full for the one-on-one health consulting with Flora. It was deeper than her desire to lose weight. It was about her emotional attachment and relationship to food, and her relationship with herself.

Food is one of the most powerful drugs in our world. It is also medicine. Eating can be a route to heal, or a way of soothing, numbing, or disconnecting. Food is a pathway to self-connection, and in all cultures, it is a bridge to celebration. When we celebrate, we eat. Sad? Eat. Happy? Eat. Having an emotion? Eat. And it's not optional for us as a species to skip out on food—we need it to survive. So, developing a healthy relationship with food is imperative.

Your relationship to food is holy. Food is sacred and can be a way to connect with a higher power. The opposite is also true. When you starve yourself or overly restrict your intake of your favorite foods, you are disconnecting from the Universe. To purge via vomiting, excessive overexercising, or engaging in an activity that disrupts your digestive system, you reinforce you are not whole—that there is something about you that is not enough or not worthy. Through food consumption, you can control your own "enoughness." And through excessive control over this bodily function of hunger, there lives a bigger belief that there will be an "end" or a finish line in sight that will equate to "enoughness." Maybe it's the exact number on the scale. Maybe it's comments from other people. In any case, this false end goal strips you of your God-given right to trust yourself, feel powerful, and honor your own life source.

Please note: *If you are struggling with an eating disorder or obstacle, please seek help from a mental-health-care professional, as I know this can be a confronting topic.*

While working with clients on their wellness goals, I learned that half of the protocol is knowing about basic nutrition to heal your gut, clear your skin, or feel the best in your body. Your relationship to your fork also matters. Every day, you get to decide how you take care of yourself through breakfast, lunch, dinner, dessert, and snacks.

When we are born into this world, our first basic instinct is to go toward our mother's nipple. Having something in our mouths soothes us—our society has an oral fixation, if you will. It is why we chew gum, love a crunchy snack, drink coffee, then water, then tea. It's soothing to have something occupying our mouths. We kiss our lovers, chew on toothpicks and ice. We bite the insides of our cheeks or our nails, smoke, lick our lips. We learned as babies, through feedings, and through sucking on a pacifier or bottle or sucking our thumb, that filling our mouths is comforting.

What we don't learn as babies is that at some point in our lives we have to develop a healthy relationship with food and learn other routes to soothe rather than putting something in our mouth. To support someone on their wellness journey, you must first understand the psychology of eating. I started to explore psychology and the power of habit, ritual, and emotional regulation. I wanted to help people and believed that educating people on proper nutrition was one of the surest ways to transform someone's life. There are many wonderful nutrition certifications and degrees, and over the past months working with Flora, I had enjoyed consuming diverse books, podcasts, and documentaries on holistic wellness. I felt well informed about how to cater to my personal wellness goals.

But I knew that even though you might have the information, that doesn't mean change will happen.

How you feed your body (or how you don't) is a form of self-love.

Geneen Roth's book *Women Food and God,* was a major eye-opener for me. I read it while leading a teen tour through Israel, right after undergrad. Roth believes that we use food as a drug instead of dealing with our inner issues and our deepest dreams, and that there has to be more to a happy and satisfied life than a Lou Malnati's Pizzeria cookie skillet and a thigh gap. So, we eat. We eat to fill a void in our heart. We eat to soothe, we eat to celebrate, we eat to survive.

I got into this wellness world because everyone around me had a distorted relationship with food. I did Weight Watchers when I was sixteen. Since then, I have been vegan, raw vegan, Paleo, keto, plant-based, juice cleansed, and parasite cleansed. I did the cabbage soup diet before prom in high school and followed a calorie tracking app throughout college. I have restricted, and I have binged. I have counted points, macros, carbs, and calories. And here's the thing—I'm not unique. Dieting, counting carbs, and restricting calories—it's become a birth-right to so many people.

Today, I have a healthy relationship with food. I buy produce at local farm-ers' markets when possible, order some produce online, and am immersing myself in the regenerative farming movement. At mealtimes I eat with gusto, looking forward to breakfast, lunch, and dinner. I use food as a way of showing myself love and take time with my food. I like it quiet when I eat and sit crisscross applesauce (cross-legged). I use my brainpower to write, launch certification programs, and educate my clients and the people in my community about East-ern ritual and Western psychology—instead of using my brain power to count calories. I have a healthy relationship with food. There are two main reasons for this: One, I learned what nourishes me at my core. Two, I diversified my palate through travel. I eat to nourish. I breathe before I consume, nourishing myself with meals that look pretty on the outside and feel good on the inside. So much in my life changed when my relationship to food changed. And now, it's all about nourishment.

THE SCIENCE OF NOURISHMENT: WHAT NOURISHES YOU?

Nourishment looks different for every single person. In Dr. David Elkins's book *Beyond Religion,* he discusses the eight diverse paths to the sacred. There is an in-depth exercise wherein he guides you to reflect on all the past nourishing experiences you have had in your life in order to inform what you should implement now to live a nourishing life. The past informs the present. I love Dr. Elkins's model because it is not one-size-fits-all. I also enjoy reflecting on the moments in the past when I felt awe, joy, and moments of deep peace.

Nourishment doesn't just come from food; it comes from soul-expansive moments, feeling-states, and experiences.

We crave an intimate relationship with Self, with nature, and with the surrounding community. We want to feel connected. Some of us are most nourished when we are learning. Others love it when people ask them questions. When our work, daily activities, loving relationships, or intimate conversations nourish us, that shifts how we feed ourselves. When we are fulfilled, we don't need food as the stimulating factor in our lives. We don't need food to fill the void in our soul where community, connection, and self-love should be. That is why my live events are called NOURISH, because that feeling-state encompasses all we crave.

JOURNAL PROMPTS

Defining True Nourishment

Write down five of your most nourishing memories ever. When was the last time you had a conversation with someone that lit you up? When was the last time you felt awe? Write down your memory of a meal you had with family or friends where you left feeling fulfilled. Write down a memory you have of when you overate or underate. What did you really need in that moment? What does true nourishment mean to you? What must occur today for you to feel nourished tomorrow?

SPICE UP YOUR LIFE

Diversifying your palate means eating foods outside the norm of your culture or the place you live. If you've ever had the feeling of understimulation or complete indifference around mealtime, it's time to explore meal roulette. You may not yet have had your best meal ever!

Meal roulette is when you spin a physical globe of the world and put your finger down. Whatever country your finger lands on is the cuisine you will have for your next meal. This means going to the store to buy the ingredients for a new recipe or trying out a new restaurant. This is fun to do with family and friends, and it's a great way to introduce yourself to foods that may excite and nourish you. Get curious! If your finger lands on a country you've never explored or haven't heard much about, get on Google and explore their fare. This becomes a fun, yummy game!

I am a travel-to-eat type of girl. I am also a homebody. This dichotomy has inspired me to become a creative chef. Now I know how to make my favorite dal coconut lentils, and my signature tahini dressing and lamb *siniyah*. These are foods that light me up because they taste so good *and* offer me the feeling-state of nourishment.

Many of us have gotten into a cycle of eating a regimented diet—foods typical of our culture or what is accessible in shops or markets close to home. If this sounds like you, become an active participant in your own meal planning. You can grow herbs such as basil, mint, oregano, parsley, or rosemary indoors in indirect sunlight, and you can add them to whatever dish you're preparing. They will spice up your food and can make every meal an adventure.

MINDFUL EATING MEDITATION

This is one of my favorite practices to share on retreats. You can explore this solo or in company with others. Start practicing mindful eating with just yourself and then notice how the practice can shift when in company. Remember this meditation whenever you want to feel more connected to your plate when you are eating. It is a digestible tool to bring yourself to the present moment in a calmer headspace.

Sit down at a beautifully laid table, perhaps with flowers or a lit candle in the center. Take a moment to feel comfortable and honor the ether that surrounds you—the space between you and your table, the space between your water glass and your plate. Notice your posture. Ideally, the height of the table feels comfortable, and there is no need for you to hunch over while you are dining. Are you comfy? Do what you need to do to be as comfortable as possible. How do your clothes feel on your body? Is your sweater itchy? Are your pants too loose or too tight? If so, change your outfit to reach a peak level of comfort before your meal.

After you have plated your meal, look at your food. Notice the different colors. Pay attention to what you are most excited to eat first. Do any specific feeling-states come up for you? Are you excited? Hungry? Smell the fresh aromas. Do they bring back any memories? Describe to yourself what the food smells like to you. Can you imagine what it tastes like before you take your first bite?

If you are dining with others, take notice of the conversation. I have observed that when I am listening to intense topics during a meal, it affects my mindful eating experience. Is the TV on? Is there music playing? The intended focus in this practice is a relaxed environment for you to enjoy your meal. So, change things accordingly. Adjust the lighting if the room feels too bright or dim.

Pick up your utensils. Feel the weight of them in your hands. Bring your utensils to the plate and cut and prepare your first bite. Bring the bite to your lips—feel the texture on your lips. Place the food in your mouth. How does this first bite feel in your mouth? How does it taste? Chew slowly. Eat your meal in a way that feels intuitive, natural. If you notice yourself eating quickly, take a deep breath. Slow down. Maintain an awareness of your breath while you eat. Observe any potent emotions that may have come up for you.

When you have finished your meal, pay attention to your digestion. Did the slowing down and experiencing your meal feel nourishing to your body?

JOURNAL PROMPTS

Exploring Mindful Eating

During the practice, did you want to eat faster? What did you notice about your food that you have never observed before? What did you have to shift to feel comfy?

EAT WITH YOUR HANDS

While living in Mumbai, I was integrated into Indian culture and ate every meal with my hands. Many cultures consume their food without cutlery. Maybe you've noticed the difference in taste and texture when you eat with your hands versus utensils. If you want to foster a new relationship with your plate, try eating with your hands. (Just wash your hands and clean under your fingernails before and afterward!) This is also a wonderful way to enjoy mealtime with your kids, because they love having the chance to feel different textures and temperatures of their food.

PRAYER AND INTENTION

All organized religions have a blessing statement before meals. Many of these are rooted in gratitude to their specific God and to the land or the recent harvest. Before consuming your meal, take a moment to bless yourself and to bless your food. This moment of prayer marks the threshold between the mundane and the sacred.

When leading retreats, I encourage participants to be silent during break-fast. No matter where the retreats are—Chicago, Costa Rica, Israel, India—the morning silence remains consistent. This is a time for participants to wake up slowly, relax into the retreat culture space, and connect with the food on their plate in their own way. This silence becomes a prayer to consume food from a place of peace. At this moment, you can co-create with the energy around you through your food, consume something healthful and nourishing, and bless it in your own way.

Choose a blessing that feels aligned with you. Consider this: When you bless your food, you are charging it energetically with your good wishes and inten-tions. Then you consume the thing you are blessing, and your body processes it and uses it to nourish your cells. Your blessings of good intentions for your food matter. They transform every meal into a ceremony.

EMBODIMENT EXERCISE: BLESS YOUR FOOD

Create a prayer for blessing your food. To whom do you need to offer gratitude for the food on your plate? Perhaps the Universe who created it, Mother Nature who grew it, the land that nourished it, the farmers who tended and picked it, the truckers who transported it, the grocers who sold it, whomever bought it, etc.

What intention are you charging into your food?

Mark time. Is there something that you are celebrating? Perhaps you have guests at your dinner table or you are celebrating a wonderful week or the start of a new day.

After blessing your food, check in. Take a deep breath. This allows you to consume your meal from a place of "rest and digest." This technique allows your food to digest better and is an emotional regulation technique. From a relaxed state, consume your blessed food.

COFFEE MEDITATION

Many people start their morning with a hot beverage. Perhaps it's coffee or tea for energy, a calming broth, or warm lemon water. Whatever your drink of choice, this calming practice will relax and energize you for the day ahead. This meditation combines breathwork, which relaxes the nervous system, intention (for when you visualize the best possible outcome of the day), and a ceremony wherein you bless your drink and then consume it. Please practice this every morning with your hot beverage or when the situation calls for it. For those of you with full schedules, this may align well with your day-to-day life.

Pour your hot beverage into a mug that feels comfy in your hands. Allow the warmth of the mug to warm your hands.

Close your eyes and connect with your breath. Visualize the best-case scenario for the day ahead. Picture yourself moving through the tasks of your day, the people involved, and your wish for all of it to be of the highest good.

Ask yourself: "How do I desire to show up today?" Answer the question with an intention. "I intend to ..." Infuse that intention into your drink.

Offer gratitude to the producers of your beverage, the distribution that brought it to the café or place you are in, and the artist who created the mug holding it.

Holding the mug in both hands, bring it to your nose. Inhale the aroma. Feel the warmth of the steam inside your nose—perhaps the stream of air is warming the back of your throat.

Exhale through your mouth into the mug. Allow the steam to warm your face. Let the steam flowing from the mug warm your eyes. (Proceed with caution—this is a hot beverage.) Continue this breathing for a few breaths.

Notice how you feel. Enjoy your drink. Carry on with your day.

DRINK WATER

Just as a houseplant needs water to survive, so do you. So please, go drink some water. So many of us go through our days dehydrated. Water is an incredible element that supports many healthful functions in our bodies. Try to stay hydrated throughout the day. I recommend drinking two glasses of room temperature water upon waking up in the morning. This will hydrate your body and prepare you for a bowel movement. Add in minerals to support water absorption, such as a dash of high-quality salt, a squeeze of citrus, or a splash of coconut water. These extra ingredients add electrolytes, antioxidants, and minerals to support hydration.

GET FRESH AIR AND SUNSHINE

Just as a houseplant needs water, it also needs sunshine. Get outside. Sunshine is healing. When there is sun outside, try your best to get exposed to it. Get a few rays of sunshine and some natural vitamin D. Even in the winter, make sure you're getting outside in nature. These basic practices are so simple, but they are often transformational and can also be the most nourishing.

GUIDED INTEGRATION

True nourishment is the key to living a happy and joyful life. Nourishment means focusing on what fills you up emotionally and also honoring a balanced relationship with food. It is vital to foster a healthful relationship to nourishment, as it supports us in living our fullest life.

- ✺ Consider your relationship with food. Do you have most meals communally or alone? Do you celebrate with food or comfort yourself with it? Are there things you'd like to change about how you approach your meals? Pay attention to when you use food as a route to soothe as opposed to satisfying a hunger cue.

- ✺ Explore what feels soul nourishing for you. Reflect on experiences that nourished you in the past and led to feeling-states of awe, peace, and connection. Notice if you want to schedule in more experiences like that now.

- ✺ Try mindful eating. Take time with food. Notice it. Slow down during meal times and savor this connection to your plate.

- ✺ Get creative and try new cuisines. There are so many delicious types of foods to explore. And most cities have restaurants featuring cuisines from all over the world—Nepal, El Salvador, Vietnam, Ethiopia. . . . You'd be surprised how many options are out there. Get out of your comfort zone and nourish your body with new, exciting foods.

nothing can stop you

❋ Connect to your morning hot drink. My go-to coffee meditation is what I practice when I am leading retreats or have a full schedule to offer myself some breath and peace. Try this practice with your next hot bev.

❋ You are a houseplant with more complicated emotions. Make sure to water yourself by staying hydrated with electrolytes and getting time outside in the sunshine. These basic needs will lead to enhanced health.

CHAPTER 12

honoring
sacred
cycles

Like all sciences and all valuations, the psychology of women has hitherto been
considered only from the point of view of men.

—KAREN HORNEY, FEMININE PSYCHOLOGY

Imagine that in a previous life you're a menstruating woman living circa 1800 BC. You look up at the sky and see a bright full moon. You check in with yourself and notice that you have more energy than other days of the month. As you see the moon glow, you feel a charge of inspiration to use the moonlight to manifest your deepest desires and dreams. The brightness of the moon sheds such a beautiful light on the world around you. Although in your world you don't call realizing your dreams manifestation, when there is a full moon you feel inspired, awakened, perhaps even aroused. You look at your reflection in a nearby lake and you look dewy—because you are also glowing like the moon. With this extra light outside you contemplate sneaking into your lover's tent to satisfy your desires, but you decide to spend time with your sisters instead, talking about your wishes.

About two weeks go by, and the earth is quiet. When you look outside at night you see an empty moon. It is dark. The stars shine. The moon is new and doesn't show its face. As the moon rests, you decide to as well. You receive your bleed and make your way toward the Red Tent. This is where your cousins, sisters, and friends all gather during their bleed. The entire community is synced up to the same cycle. The Red Tent is warm, filled with comfortable pillows, blankets, and candles. Your aunts and grandmother prepare a warm meal to offer you. You sit down next to your cousin and bleed together into the earth, side by side. You are offering your womb to the womb of Mother Earth.

During your menstruation cycle, you rest and dream. You partake in little to no activity. You receive clarity on ideas you had earlier in the weeks when you had more energy. While braiding each other's hair, resting on pillows, and making art, you talk to your sisters and cousins about the sleeping dreams they are having, and about the boys becoming men in your community. Your mother and your aunties check in to see how you're feeling, offering oils for you to rub into your stomach and broths for you to drink. You feel well rested and taken care of. When your cycle concludes, you leave the Red Tent feeling rejuvenated and ready to embark on the month ahead.

From generation to generation, women have come together during their cycles to heal, align, and grow. Our ancestors would support different milestones and rites of passage through the metaphysical "Red Tent." *The Red Tent* is a bestselling book written by Anita Diamant that shares a retelling of ancient womanhood. The term "Red Tent" is a metaphor for the community women held with each other. Somewhere along the way, the feminine embodiment practices got watered down or even forgotten. The Red Tent was a sacred space where women would connect. This is where women would gather to birth their babies into the world and rest postpartum. This is where women would learn about their menstruation cycles by examining their older sisters and mothers moving through their own rites of passage. The Red Tent became the safe space for women to discuss certain rituals, ceremonies, and crafts. It was a harbor for exchanging wisdom, best practices, and tips on how to take care of Self and a growing family.

Our modern culture does not support our connecting with the earth in this way, in connecting with our fellow women. It doesn't slow down when we need to take a break; it doesn't seem to value our support of other women during their changes of need based on their monthly phases. There is a lot we are missing out on in the name of progress and modernity; however, incorporating our sacred cycles into our modern, day-to-day lives can help ground us and actually help make our lives more harmonious. In this chapter, I will encourage you to track your menstrual cycle (or your partner's) as well as the phases of the moon and notice how your energy changes as these phases move through you.

Menstruating women are powerful. We feel differently based on where we are in our cycle. Consciously working with our twenty-eight-day cycle, also known as the infradian rhythm, has a slew of benefits, according to Alisa Vitti, author of *Woman Code*. It can help reduce stress, promote a healthful weight, support hormonal imbalances, and improve mood. Vitti shares the hormone balancing practice of cycle syncing. Cycle syncing is for menstruating women who are not on any form of hormonal birth control who want to live a lifestyle in sync with their hormones.

Women, we are the most privileged we have ever been. The reason many of us are just now hearing about cycle syncing is because there are finally female scientists getting curious about these topics, researching them, and sharing their findings.

There are four phases in a woman's cycle: the days below are approximations and will vary with each person. Please consult a healthcare professional for medical insights, as these are general guidelines and should be treated as such. This is based on Vitti's framework and I have also added my own personal practices.

THE INFRADIAN CYCLE

Follicular Phase

Seven to ten days in length post-bleed

Hormones start off low from menstruation and then rise. Multiple eggs develop in the body and only one mature egg, the best for fertilization, is selected by the intelligence of the body to be released during ovulation, the next phase. Estrogen levels increase and the uterus lining thickens so it can hold the mature egg in the luteal phase.

During this phase, you have a lower body temperature. As it moves out of the hibernation, or rest, energy increases. Libido increases, and you may feel clear-headed. This can be a more social time where you are eager to go out into the world, meet friends, and be active. If you experience symptoms of sadness during your bleed, you may feel calm and happier now. This is the phase of new beginnings, a time to look at the month ahead and plan your events and work schedule. Business planning, team meetings, and organizing the month or year ahead can be powerful during this time. It may feel good to incorporate cardio and strength training into your movement routine.

Practice Snapshot Manifestation during this time, as it will shed light on the aligned actions you need to take. Make a point to schedule some Soul Time so your goals and dreams will become a reality. Put yourself in a new situation that excites you and feels nourishing. Are you taking time to schedule in your strengths? This is a great time to implement that practice.

KAPALABHATI BREATHING

This advanced yogic practice is best known for detoxing the body, increasing mental strength, and clearing brain fog. It is a powerful, active exercise.

Before you start, you may want to blow your nose, as this practice involves short, passive inhales and quick, active exhales through the nose. Keep your mouth closed for the duration of the exercise.

Sit in a comfortable position. If you are seated on the floor, place a bolster or pillow under your tailbone to realign your spine. This may feel like rotating your pelvic floor forward internally. No need to exaggerate a straight spine—this is just a slight opening of the hips. If this posture does not bring you comfort, you can sit on a chair.

Inhale through your nose with little effort and then do a short and forceful exhale through your nose while sucking your belly button toward your spine. You may sound like a dog panting. Do this for thirty seconds.

Pause and notice how you feel. If you feel lightheaded or dizzy, resume your normal breathing. Once you are comfortable with this practice you can increase the duration of the quick breaths to ninety-second sessions.

JOURNAL PROMPTS

Harnessing Increased Energy

As my energy increases, what do I want to focus on? Is there an event I would love to do with friends? With increased energy and while looking at the months ahead, how can I show up for myself in a big way and plan accordingly?

Ovulation

One day, typically in the middle of your cycle

Estrogen peaks and the mature egg is released into the fallopian tubes. Testosterone surges and the uterine lining continues to thicken due to estrogen. If sex occurs during this time or near the end of the follicular phase, sperm can travel to meet the egg in the fallopian tubes and fertilize it. Fertilized or not, the egg travels to the uterus. Due to rising estrogen levels, the body creates an egg white–like, slippery mucus from the vagina which can aid in conception. If you are on hormonal birth control or some hormonal IUDs, you may not ovulate.

This is the main event. This is where the magic happens! Biologically, we are designed to procreate. Ovulation hormones may shift your scent and you may even appear more attractive. Your hair and skin can be shinier, and you have increased energy. This is a time where it is easy to perform, be out in the world, and attend social gatherings or host dinner parties. If you are single and looking to attract your soulmate, dating during ovulation may feel in alignment.

This is the time to ask for that raise, pitch a new idea or project, organize your speaking engagements, run a marathon, attend a group workout class, or be a social butterfly. High-intensity workouts and training are more achievable. Typically, you feel good, maybe even less stressed. It can feel easier to tap into a flow state, connect with your inner guru, and align with your best version of Self. You are most fertile during this time and may feel more aroused. If you desire to get pregnant, this is the time to have sex.

If you do not wish to conceive, use effective precautions. Some non-hormonal options are condoms, the copper IUD, and vaginal diaphragms (although those are still proven to not be 100 percent effective). Cycle syncing is also associated with the rhythm method, an alternative to hormonal birth control that has proven quite effective when done correctly. There are new apps on the market that pair cycle tracking with taking your temperature each day to dial in on exactly when you're most likely to be ovulating. You can also pee on an ovulation strip to confirm if you're in fact ovulating.

TANTRIC BREATHING
PARTNER PRACTICE

Tantra is a sacred lineage of yogic teachings focused on connection. If you are in partnership and desire to connect through breathwork, try this practice.

Person A sits down on a couch or bed facing Person B.

Person B sits on Person A's lap, facing them.

Person A wraps their arms around Person B, using their legs connected to the earth as a sturdy base. Person B wraps their arms and legs around Person A, sitting on Person A's lap.

Both place their heads together, foreheads touching.

When Person A inhales through the nose, Person B syncs up with them, inhaling too.

Both also sync up on exhales through the nose.

Repeat this practice for three minutes or until you feel ready to move on.

Optional: During the practice, you can massage the other person's back, or rub their ears or scalp. The focus of the practice is connection.

SELF-PLEASURE

Use your hand or a toy. Your aim can be to achieve orgasm or to self-massage and connect to your pleasure center.

JADE OR YONI EGG

This is the practice of placing a high-quality egg-shaped crystal inside your vagina, in the same way you would insert a menstruation cup. Make sure you're using an approved Yoni Egg from a reputable company. Please sanitize the Yoni Egg before use (and after). You can start with quick sessions of noticing this connection within you and even work your pelvic floor.

Note: If you have a history of pelvic floor dysfunction such as incontinence, pain during intercourse, or bladder urgency/frequency, please consult a pelvic floor therapist before use.

The key focus here is to recognize when you clench. For example, your body is always communicating with you. Let's say you are reading over a menu debating what to have for dinner and then you see a grass-fed burger on the menu and you clench. It is as if you're "turned on," or you are having a guttural reaction to that food. Pay attention here. This connection will feel more obvious with a Yoni Egg in place.

JOURNAL PROMPTS

Celebrating an Upswing or Peak

When you feel good, what are three desires you have? What turns you on? What lights you up?

Luteal Phase

Ten to fourteen days in length between ovulation and your bleed
The uterine lining thickens to provide a secure and nourishing place for a fertilized egg. If conception did not occur, then the unfertilized egg disintegrates within twenty-four hours and the uterus prepares to shed it in the next phase. Progesterone, the pro-gestation hormone, peaks during this phase.

This is a time to focus on what feels comfy and cozy. Cleaning up around the house, tidying the closet, or completing organizational chores may feel good during this time. If you wrote, pitched a project, or created art in the prior weeks, now is the time to go check your progress. This is a good time for editing and restructuring. You may feel sensitive during this time, so it's not the best time for intense conversations or a feedback review with your boss. If your hormones are imbalanced, you may experience feeling-states of sadness or anxiety. PMS may occur during this time. Alisa Vitti suggests that by living a phase-based cycle, partaking in healthful eating and lifestyle practices, PMS symptoms can decrease dramatically.

This is the time to do chores around the house that allow you to relax during your bleed, and to wrap up projects at work. To keep balanced, it is best to eat more calories from real whole foods during this time. Focus on slower movements like yoga, barre, gentle strength training, and beginner-friendly hikes.

ABHYANGA

Abhyanga is an Ayurvedic oil-based massage. Heat a high-quality coconut, avocado, or olive oil on the stove on low heat and then massage your whole body, focusing on long strokes and smaller circular motions near crevices and joints. You can do this solo or with a partner.

CARD PULLING

Intuition can increase during this time, and working with a deck that you feel drawn to can be powerful! Find a deck that feels most in alignment with you. After shuffling the deck, fan the cards out in front of you. Ask a question that is on your heart. Pull a card. Notice how the card offers guidance. This is also a wonderful time to reflect on any symbolism in the cards that may be coming up for you in your dreams or in your day-to-day activities. Meditate with the card you pulled. Pause. What comes through?

MORNING PAGES

The concept of mornings pages was brought to the world in author Julia Cameron's bestselling book *The Artist's Way*. Morning pages is the practice of waking up in the morning and jotting down anything that's on your mind. Cameron believes that the practice of morning pages is a low-stress way to express yourself and release any thoughts or fears that are in the way of showing up for your fullest expression of creativity.

JOURNAL PROMPTS

Taking a Beat

Is there an idea you had earlier in the week you'd like to circle back to now? Focusing on details is great during this phase; however, do you notice your inner perfectionist popping in? If so, what does this voice sound like or say? Do you want to nest by yourself or cuddle up with a partner? If so, when can you schedule that in?

Menstrual Phase

Days one (first day of bleeding) to seven of your bleed
The menstruation phase is when blood and other fluids flow from the vagina. This is a shedding of the uterine lining. Hormones are at their lowest during this phase.

The right and left brain can communicate more clearly. It may feel best to spend time with fewer people, or with people for whom you don't need to perform. It may also feel good to spend time solo. You may feel cuddly during this time and desire the feeling-state of calmness. This is a wonderful time to reflect on the month that has passed and to integrate any emotionally charged experiences. There is a different type of clarity and rawness during this phase. It may be a good idea to reflect on a decision and make sure it feels in alignment.

Working too much during this phase may not feel in alignment. Feeling-states of overwork and stress can sometimes lead to an emotional (and often necessary) release. This is a good time to focus on calming yin yoga, slow movements, progressive muscle relaxation, and body scans, where you bring your attention to specific areas of the body and gently breathe into them. Eating high-quality red meat during this phase may feel good. Try to do less, rest, and take it as easy. Allow yourself to dream and consider the best-case scenario. Write with a red pen. Wear red clothes. Connect to the color red.

LET GO

If you notice yourself holding on to an emotion, person, or event that still doesn't sit well with you, consider this visualization. As you bleed, as the blood leaves your body, picture the emotion, person, or event leaving your womb space.

FEAR INVENTORY

This was a powerful practice for me when I was feeling anxious before I moved to India; use it whenever you are having consistent fear-based thoughts. Set a timer for three minutes and write your fear-based thoughts and feelings on a piece of paper. Once the timer goes off, light your favorite candle and set it in a clear, safe space in front of you. (Have a jug of water on hand for safety.) Use a prayer or mantra that feels empowering to you to burn and release your fears. Here is one you can borrow if it feels aligned: "I honor the version of myself that has these fears and wants to keep me safe. I choose to see love instead of this fear and trust myself and the Universe. Show me how good it can get." Then use the flame from the candle and light the paper on fire. (I recommend doing this over the kitchen sink to prevent a fire hazard.)

STILLNESS MEDITATION

Embody a stillness meditation, like the Rainbow Meditation in Chapter 5 or the release practice in Chapter 2. Or take a moment to lie down on the floor. Take up space, opening up your armpits and legs, allowing your lymph nodes to breathe. Close your eyes. Take a moment to notice your breath. Practice a gentle inhale for five counts and exhale for five counts. Keep this gentle practice for up to five minutes. You are welcome to drift off to sleep from here.

YIN YOGA LEG SWAY

This calming practice will relax the body and bring in light, intuitive stretches.

To start, lie on your back, in bed, on the floor, or on a yoga mat. Get comfortable. Place a pillow under your head and cover yourself with a blanket.

Pull your knees toward your chest in ball pose. Bring your feet up and plant them on the ground. Then let your knees sway left and right like windshield wipers.

Continue to sway your legs, breathing into your lower belly. Try to visualize this breath flowing in and out of the womb space.

If swaying to one side feels good, drop your legs and continue breathing. Honor intuitive movements and pause for about a minute on each side.

To conclude, stretch your legs long. Inhale and pull your legs back to center, and then back into ball pose.

Continue with your day or take a nap! Whatever feels good.

WOMB TO WOMB

Body to earth, earth to body. Just like our ancestors in the Red Tent, you can honor this lineage by bleeding into the earth. Wear a dress or skirt with nothing underneath. Go to Mama Earth, sit down, and free bleed. Visualize yourself sitting in the Red Tent with your loved ones and embrace any wisdom that may channel through. Bring a paper and pen and write down any clarifying moments, epiphanies, or emotions that arise.

MENSTRUATION CUP RITUAL

The ability to bleed and still move throughout our everyday tasks is an incredible innate power of women. Our cycle makes us superhuman. If you want to get more witchy, try this practice.

Just as we observe our urine to see if we are sufficiently hydrated or our bowel movements to notice if we are constipated or regular, period blood is another biological tool that can help us understand our state of wellness. If you find the next practice icky, I invite you to investigate why. Note: Please use a menstruation cup for these rituals. If you are squeamish from blood, skip this practice altogether.

While you are in the shower, pour the menses from your menstruation cup into your hand. Take a moment to observe your period blood—its color, its texture. Are there any clumps? Is it pure liquid? Connect deeply to this function of your body.

Bless yourself. Massage your menses around your navel using long, circular motions. The third chakra is at the navel. This is the place where we connect to who we are at our core and where we act on our desires and belief systems. Breathe into this space.

Chant your "I am" statements.

Think about the aligned actions you are taking on your dreams (Soul Time).

Move into your Snapshot Manifestation.

When you have completed these steps, wash your stomach and notice the red color of your period mixed with shower water flow down the drain. Picture these fluids moving into mother earth planting the seeds to your deep wishes and desires. There is a sacred story passed through oral tradition that when you hear of civilization in barren areas like on top of mountains and in deserts, it is because the women gave their blood back to Mother Earth for fertilization. If you feel connected with this idea, pour your menses into a glass jar, dilute it with water, and mix. Use this concoction on your houseplants or garden as fertilizer.

CYCLE STACKING

I am best known as a spiritual psychology and meditation teacher and business coach. One of my favorite things to teach when supporting purpose-driven entrepreneurs is the practice of stacking your personal and business schedule. It goes like this:

First, organize your yearly business plan. This includes your launch calendar, when programs begin or end, planned events like speaking gigs, conferences, and retreats.

Once your calendar is set, take out your period tracking app or whatever you use to track your cycle.

If possible, try to plan your launches, big meetings, presentations, and speaking gigs during ovulation or during your cycle when you have more energy.

Start stacking. For me, this looks like having my client-facing coaching calls all on one day a week, perhaps on a Tuesday, so I am staying focused on showing up as a guide all day. I enjoy setting aside one day a week for connecting with my team and organizing the backend tasks for my businesses. Stacking has been a profound tool for content creation and staying aligned with creativity, because I can stay in that energy rather than shifting from one headspace to another or one task to another.

JOURNAL PROMPTS

Releasing

Is there something that is not sitting well with you that you desire to let go of? What must happen for you to feel your comfiest and coziest during this phase? What fear-based thoughts have come up for you, and how can you choose to release them?

SHINE BRIGHTLY LIKE THE MOON

Some of us have a new moon resonance, while others track more with the full moon. The key is to sync just by observing. Wherever you live in the world, before you go to sleep, take a moment to look out your window at the sky. Notice the shape of the moon, its color, and where it sits in the sky, and check in with how you feel. Journal your feelings. Do this over a series of months and you will see a personalized pattern emerging. Write down some observations in your journal.

NEW AND FULL MOON SACRED CODES

Because of our lifestyles, our rhythms shift based on how we are eating and sleeping and how much stress we experience day to day. For myself, when I travel often, my cycle shifts. Choose which rituals you desire to embody either on the full or new moon. Keep in mind that if something needs more light, it's better to do the ritual during the full moon. If it needs more contemplation or inner work, that is new moon energy.

BIRTHDAY CANDLE RITUAL

If you need a pick-me-up, try this practice. Create an "I am" statement for your day. Light a birthday candle (or any type of clean candle). Inhale through your nose. Hold the vision of what it looks like when you move through your day, embodying your "I am" statement. On your exhale, blow out the candle as if you are making a wish.

CREATE AN EARTH ALTAR

Create an earth altar to help you ground your deepest desires and dreams into the physical world. Fill a large bowl with diverse elements that light you up. I use a wooden bowl filled with crystals I mined with Jon in Arkansas, curly seashells from Costa Rica, red string for Jerusalem, and rocks from beaches around the world. You can add anything that resonates with you. Write on a piece of paper what you're manifesting and place it in the bowl as well. Place the bowl on your earth altar and allow it to sit and rest. Trust that the dreams you wrote down will be planted and grow roots to thrive into your reality.

Optional: Place your written desires underneath your pillow. Sleep on your note for a couple nights to infuse your dreams with your manifestations, then transfer it to your earth altar.

CREATE YOUR OWN RITUAL

Create your own ritual by choosing what resonates with you and going from there. Choose today to look out the window, connect to how you feel in the moon's presence, and move into a DIY ritual. Empower yourself through trusting in your inner guru. Know that whatever you choose to do is going to be the best and most personalized route for you!

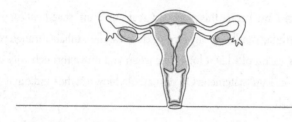

GUIDED INTEGRATION

Getting in touch with our sacred cycles is grounding, and it can help us self-regulate and anticipate potential bursts of productivity and phases when rest is required. If you desire to connect more deeply to yourself or a partner who menstruates, start paying attention to the ebbs and flows of energy during the month.

> ☀ **Try connecting with each of the four phases of the infradian cycle with an exercise from this chapter.** Remember, women typically have more energy during the follicular and ovulation phases, feel nesty and practice organization in the luteal phase, and ground plus rest during menstruation.

nothing can stop you

✹ **Notice whether the phases of the moon line up with how you're feeling.** If something needs more light and clarity, the brightness of the full moon is a great time to connect. If something needs quiet and darkness, then the new moon may feel in alignment.

✹ **Honor your lineage.** So many of us come from diverse backgrounds, and yet the theme that remains consistent is that all women have their bleed. Choose any of the practices or rituals from this chapter to mark time, and perhaps ask your mother, aunties, sisters, and grandmothers what they do, or did, to honor their cycle.

CHAPTER 13

when authentic people come together, the world heals

*One of the scariest things in our lives
is actually doing what we know we want to do.*

—CHERYL STRAYED

"Why did I have to be this type of person?" my client Tania shared with me at the end of our call. "Why do I constantly feel like I need to push my boundaries, be outside my comfort zone, and do things so differently?" She sighed loudly, allowing some of the stress to leave her chest.

We were discussing her plans for an upcoming solo trip to Europe and then Asia, where she'd be working remotely and creating a coaching business on the side. I knew this feeling deeply. So often our soulmate clients are a mirror of our past version of Self. There have been many moments in which I've been upset with myself for being this type of person too. On many sleepless nights, I lay awake in my parents' house, in my childhood bedroom, counting down the days before a big flight across the world. I'd think, *Why did I think I could do this? So much can go wrong! Why do I always have to push myself so far outside my comfort zone?* Those days leading up to big trips were always filled with extreme anxiety and fear. In those moments, I leaned into my inner guru for guidance and comfort.

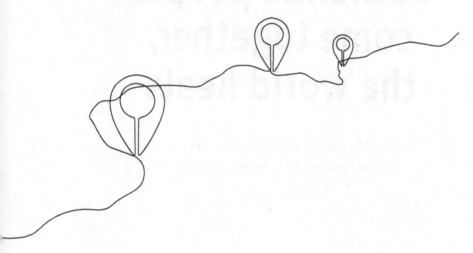

However, choosing your big desire is the most crucial act. There may be a societal conditioning where people, or close loved ones, will say, "Isn't this enough? Isn't your life enough at this point?" And this can lead to feelings of guilt for wanting more—more adventure, more orgasmic meals, more soul-expanding conversations with people who truly *get* you. Yes, it is so good to be grateful for what you have and to celebrate the simple pleasures in life. And you are more than welcome to pursue the deep calling even if it scares you to live life on the edge. Also, it is important to be surrounded by others who are willing to do the needed work to live their fullest lives, who look at you and understand this feeling-state, as opposed to judging you or encouraging you to conform and be content with what is.

Living life on the edge looked different for me based on where I was in the world. When I woke up feeling lonely in my apartment in Mumbai, I convinced myself to go to yoga, eat something, and get out in the world. I knew that miracles would not happen if I stayed inside all day. In Ubud, Bali, I was uncomfortable and not at all at peace—because there were cockroaches roaming my whole villa. I didn't sleep for two weeks from fear. I had this under-the-skin, dirty feeling. It was well known that the area in which my villa was located was filled with dark spirits. So, between the scary energy and the cockroaches, I stayed up all night, night after night. And then there was the time I escaped from the horny guru in Rishikesh. In these moments, I felt unsettled about my decisions to live life outside the status quo and be someone who walked a different path or challenged the typical worldview.

You have to trust this calling to take up space and pursue that adventure, which is exactly what I shared with Tania on that call. Even if something goes wrong for her, it will redirect her to a more aligned path. Even if it feels sticky for a moment, her experience will lead to miracles. When you trust in yourself and listen to your soul's calling, you begin to experience the miracles that occur along the way. My miracles included letting my loneliness in Mumbai lead me to a trendy cocktail bar, where I met the most amazing people. I made a wonderful group of friends in Mumbai and had a boyfriend while I was there. My miracles led me to flee the cockroaches in Ubud and apply for a consultant and yoga teacher position at a coding school in Canggu, closer to the beach. I got the gig and spent two weeks with the most incredible people in a gorgeous, bug-free villa while also learning how to code. Dodging the advances of that horny Rishikesh guru led to me meeting soulmate friends at a more authentic and sacred yogic ashram. I later spent a week on the back of a motorcycle exploring the Himalayas! Each time I decided to pursue my soul's calling, and even if something went wrong, I was always guided to a more aligned path and met incredible people.

WHY WE CRAVE CONNECTION

I can think of many moments throughout my life when trusting my inner guru rerouted me. It also guided me to powerful soul friends. There is power in numbers. There is medicine in being seen, witnessed, and heard. The dreams on your heart are much more likely to manifest when you share them with others who are also working toward their passions. Whether it was in a dingy post-college apartment, a sacred yoga shala, a community square, or a women's meditation group, when people came together with shared desires, dreams, and wishes, miracles occurred. If you want to take up space, double your devotion, and multiply your dreams tenfold, then I recommend guiding your own gathering of like-minded, supportive people.

STARTING YOUR OWN COUNSOUL

Who you are is the sum of the five to ten people you spend most of your time with—so choose wisely. This book offers you diverse tools from both Eastern ritual and Western psychology. Take these practices "off the mat" and into your life. Immerse yourself in them. I suggest you start what I call a CounSOUL, a gathering of like-minded people who are down to do the deep work and commune on matters of the soul.

Council is when people come together to delegate, discuss, and manage certain affairs. CounSOUL is when you invite your soul friends to come together to contemplate matters of the heart. It is a place where you can speak unedited and allow your community to hold space for you. If you choose to be the host, it is your responsibility to set the tone, offer a formal invitation (yes, a text message is fine!), and create the welcoming space for others.

I recommend meeting monthly, if possible, in alignment with the new or full moon. Shift the date based on the needs of your group—the priority is meeting consistently, not following the lunar calendar. The beautiful thing about CounSOUL is that you get to personalize yours based on where you are in the world and your intention that month.

When hosting a CounSOUL, delegate diverse tasks. Share responsibility. One person can oversee food and beverages, for example, another person can set down the cushions or blankets, someone can be the greeter, and someone else can tidy up afterward.

COUNSOUL CEREMONY GUIDELINES

I suggest having a few guidelines in place to help make sure that things run smoothly.

First, no phones during the ceremony. (Of course you can take a picture before or after to share with the group or on social media. This may inspire others to host their own CounSOULs. Tag me @erinrdoppelt, I'd love to see your pictures!)

Dressing up is optional. Depending on the group, you might ask people if they want to dress up as what they want to embody, wear a color that activates them, or even wear a fun costume.

Honor the elements as much as possible as a pathway to connect with the seasons and ground the ceremony. These are just some options. Get creative here:

- ✺ Earth: Incorporate rocks, crystals, flowers, leaves, dirt, or tree branches into your ceremony.

- ✺ Fire: Light a campfire, if outside. If inside, use beeswax candles, a fireplace, or incense.

- ✺ Water: Offer warm tea to drink, wine, or cacao. Set bowls of water around, place flowers in vases filled with water, or have your event near a body of water.

- ✺ Air: Open windows. Use an air diffuser or fans indoors. Or get outside in the breeze.

- ✺ Ether: Honor what is liminal—the details of the ceremony, the space between each person, and the surrounding elements. Focus on the feeling of comfort.

Weave in your own unique flair. Trust your inner guru. The aim is to invite all participants to feel as safe as possible while also bringing in elements that only you can weave in. For example, if you love to cook, share one of your beloved recipes. If you love sacred elements (like the mandala), maybe there is a print-out mandala everyone can color during the ceremony. Perhaps you love meditation; take a meditation in this book and use it to guide your group into a peaceful state of relaxation. If you and your group align with a specific organized religion, you can integrate those customs or prayers for the group. I have guided CounSOUL circles for Shabbat, the Jewish sabbath which is the day of rest from sundown Friday to sundown Saturday, and have married the Shabbat rituals of lighting the candles, blessing the bread, and washing up to the sacred connection of that month's CounSOUL topic.

Note: You only need two people to have CounSOUL.

Dive into some of the journal prompts or embodiment practices in this book to facilitate a discussion.

HOW TO HOST A COUNSOUL

Please note, these are loose guidelines. My highest hope for you on this CounSOUL facilitation is to weave in your own brilliance through your inner guru connection and create a container that feels nourishing and unique to you.

Suggested shopping list:

❋ Candles

❋ Matches

❋ Beverage of choice

❋ Flowers

- ✺ Sacred quotes or items to place in the center or on an altar

- ✺ Mantra deck

- ✺ This book

- ✺ Crystals

- ✺ Pillows

- ✺ Materials for journaling

Greet your guests and offer them a beverage. Invite them to leave their phone either in their bag or in a specific place (so the phones can have a ceremony of their own—ideally, in another room). In almost all cultures, the welcoming drink is a custom associated with peace and nurturing. I recommend warm drinks in colder climates, as it can help relax the nervous system; it's optional to offer wine, should you desire. In many holy texts, wine is used as a resource to connect with the land or harvest. It is also a symbol of celebration. If alcohol doesn't align with you and your inner guru, or if you do not have a healthy relationship with it, skip it. You can substitute whole fruit juice, sparkling water, or any beverage you wish.

Create the circle. Sit in a circle so each person can see the faces of those around them without needing to shift their body too much. A circle during ceremony symbolizes unity. Place an altar of some sort in the center of the circle, if you wish. This can be filled with natural elements (earth, air, fire, water, ether), mantra decks, symbols with which you align, or anything you want to have charged energetically by the goodness of this gathering. For example, you can place a crystal at the center of the circle, move through the ceremony, and trust that the crystal will be infused with the wishes you shared.

Some people in your CounSOUL may be meeting for the first time, so give them space to connect. It is your job as host to introduce everyone.

Allow organic conversation to occur.

Start the CounSOUL by establishing this moment as differing from all others. For example, you can chant "Om" three times, or practice the yogic breath discussed in Chapter 2. You can guide your guests through Kapalabhati (see Chapter 12). Check in with your inner guru. Ask, What unique ritual can I share at the beginning of our ceremony that will help me relax, connect with my authentic Self, and support all participants in this circle to feel safe too? Start there.

Once the CounSOUL begins, you can dive into any of the exercises, journaling prompts, or embodiment practices in this book. The bulk of the ceremony happens here. You can offer a quotation, read a passage from this book, or offer a theme for the group to discuss. Keep this part structured—but loosely—leaving room for sharing, connection, and observation.

Ask everyone to connect regarding their desires, dreams, and manifestations. Talk about what aligned action every person in the circle will bring before your next gathering. This is suggested for two reasons: one, to support accountability; and two, to allow others to witness their dreams.

Work with the mantra "I'll have some of that!" It's a powerful manifestation statement that you can use when someone shares a desire, wish, or dream you also want to call in for yourself. It is a tool that helps you become clearer about what your heart yearns for. Use this whenever you hear something that deeply resonates and that you also want on your path.

Close your CounSOUL with a prayer of gratitude, through breathing one collective breath, or by blowing out candles and making a wish. Once your

CounSOUL is closed, no one may speak outside of the group about what was discussed or shared. The wisdom and words shared during CounSOUL are holy. It is important to keep that energy connected to just these moments of ceremony.

Have you ever had a vulnerability hangover or felt that you overshared something you were processing? It is one of the worst feelings when we speak our truth and those around us do not witness or hold our heart as we process. For CounSOUL to work, there cannot be unkind words or speaking about what was shared during the ceremony behind the sharers' backs. Only invite in those whom you know can hold their tongue post-ceremony. If you hear of someone speaking about what was shared during CounSOUL, firmly ask them to keep it to themselves. Emphasize that this container is sacred.

Once the ceremony ends, pull out phones and calendars to set the date and time for your next CounSOUL. Consistency is key. Linger in any conversations that feel nourishing.

When people with a shared goal, vision, and feeling-state come together, the world heals. These CounSOULs have the power to change your life. It's an amazing thing to pursue your dreams, and it's even better if you inspire those around you to do the same. Start with a small group. Allow it to grow. It's possible to do CounSOULs virtually, so if there are people you want to have CounSOUL with who don't live near you, hold your CounSOUL in a virtual setting.

Meeting with people all around the world has been a powerful pathway for me to expand my belief system. When you are living at the edge of your comfort zone, you meet people who see the world differently than you do. If you can, learn from them and their experiences, ask questions, and discuss diverse worldviews. When you feel as though you're the only person in your community asking specific questions or choosing a different path, you must do the needed work to meet other people thinking like you. A great way to facilitate that is by running your own CounSOUL.

GUIDED INTEGRATION

This is your reminder that your deepest desires and dreams are going to be your road map to living on your highest possible timeline. Even if something goes wrong along the way, trust that your inner guru will guide you to aligned people who support feelings of connection.

- ✸ Know that you are allowed to desire more. Try your best to find a like-minded community that will uphold your desires and not make you feel guilty for craving a different path.

- ✸ Build your close circle. Curate a close community by starting your own CounSOUL with a group of like-minded people who are willing to explore diverse rituals, speak unedited, and hold the sacredness of this container. Try to meet regularly to foster deep connection and support.

- ✸ Honor the elements. The elements are another tool you can use to drop deeper into ceremony and infuse your space with grounded, clear, and good energy. You are welcome to get creative here.

CONCLUSION

i reserve the right to change my mind

We are all just walking each other home.

—RAM DASS

And this brings me to one of our last lessons in this book: I reserve the right to change my mind.

It is an incredible thing to be curious, to explore, and to grow. As a species, we have this wonderful ability to shift. If you are on the self-help train, looking for the next superfood to eat, the next workout class to try, the next book/podcast/TED Talk/retreat/romance/insert the thing that will change your life, you need to hear this: There is nothing and no one coming to fix you, save you, or put the flame under your ass to "do the thing." Your dreams are your responsibility. If you stay on the path because you love to learn and are curious, that is wonderful; but you don't need to be "fixed." Your healing, alignment, and spiritual growth are your responsibility and require physical action along with absorbing the integrated materials. So I am begging you—trust yourself. Trust your inner guru. You know what is of highest alignment for you. Do the thing you've always wanted—you're more than ready!

I've done all the fad diets and workout classes. I've read so many self-help books, studied the memoirs of my mentors, and all who supported me at that moment. It nourished me and helped me realign. But all that curiosity led me to the most important realization of all: that I could always walk myself home, that I would always choose what was right for me, and that the best is yet to come.

And, friend, if someone challenges you or makes you feel lousy for wanting "more" out of this current human experience, remember that not everyone gets access to your dreams, nor do they need to understand. Resist the urge to defend yourself; you don't need to. You do not need to feel shame for wanting a more expansive feeling-state or explain why you desire it. Trust in your inner guru as you navigate a different path, a unique reality. Go for it! Bring this book along with you on your journey.

nothing can stop you

When you trust yourself, you know that you can do more things outside your comfort zone because you followed your inner wisdom. You trusted your truth. Your inner guru connection is the pathway to your most soul-authentic life, a life unique to you. It's your permission slip to live your life out loud to its fullest.

My greatest hope is that you choose one of the many practices and tools in this book and use it to make a huge difference in your life. Continue your Mornings with Meaning. Allow yourself space to breathe. Come back to this book again and again. Revisit the exercises and journal prompts to see how you have transformed. You will feel differently about your responses based on your headspace now and in the future. As I re-read the stories I wrote, they sometimes feel like a different person ago. This book fell out of me. It was easy to write because these are the stories and practices that guide my life and that brought me to this moment in time.

As this book comes to a close, I pray you know, in your inner being, that you can embody your inner guru. When you are living in tune with your most authentic Self through your inner guru connection, your dreams are within reach. Over time, my connection to my inner guru has shifted—we became so integrated that we became one. I am the spokesperson for my desires. I am the activator of my dreams. I so trusted my truth that I became me. To feel strong within yourself and to trust yourself is so nourishing.

I am my inner guru and my inner guru is me.

L'chaim, l'ahava, v'tuv lev. To life, to love, to a good heart. I wish you all things good, positive, and infinite. I hope you become your most authentic

Self. I honor you. Together let us bring our hands to our heart in *namaskar*. Inhale. We bring our thumb knuckles to our lips and kiss them gently, bringing our hands to our third-eye center, the point between our eyebrows. We honor our inner knowing, our inner guru connection, our innermost authentic Self. Bowing forward, we surrender, heart toward the earth, arms stretched out long. I bow to you, my reader. Thank you for being here. Your greatest work is to show up, aligned with your inner guru.

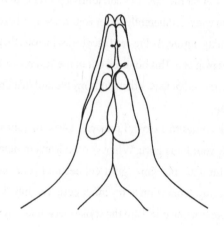

acknowledgments

Thank you, dear reader, for showing up. I have said it before and I will say it again: this is the greatest joy of my life to share this book with you. May it serve you deeply and completely. May you know, in your inner being, that the best is yet to come, and you just need to make room for the miracle. Thank you, dear reader, for doing the work. I am so inspired by you.

To my beloved soulmate, Jon. I love our life. Thank you for being the first to read and edit this book and provide loving feedback. Thank you for always holding the vision for what is possible with me. Thank you for reminding me who I am when I feel disconnected. You're my greatest manifestation come to be. I love you.

To my sister, Danielle, I am so grateful for your feedback, love, and support for this book. Loving you is what helped guide me into my devoted meditation practice. Caroline, thank you for also reading and providing commentary on this book. I love your detailed wisdom and talking big themes of this book out with you. Simone, thank you for your ability to go from woo-woo to high level academia, your wisdom is so appreciated. Stefanie, thank you for your feedback and expertise for grounding the details in Chapter 12! To my Pamela, for always being the most solid, loyal, and biggest cheerleader best friend. A win for me is a win for you.

To Jahna and Jordy, thank you for going back and forth with me on the intro of this book you both have always encouraged me to be my fullest expression of Self. To my brother, Matthew, thank you for meeting me in Israel as I was becoming who I am now and encouraging the path of the "optional challenge."

Mom and Dad, you're the best. I am so grateful my soul chose you. The reason my childhood home is a grounding and safe place of refuge is because of both of you. Thank you for always picking me up from the airport and reminding me why Chicago is the best. I love you more.

To my friends I met along the road: the way you made me feel will stick with me forever. To the strangers who showed me kindness when I was so far away from home, this book is also in honor of you. And, of course, all the yogic educators I studied under, the aligned and out of alignment ones—I learned so much from sitting in your energy. Also, to my professors at Columbia University, thank you for bridging psychology and spirituality—giving people the tools they need to heal, align, and grow. And a very special thank you to Shorashim, Israel Outdoors, and Birthright Israel for spearheading so much of my spiritual development.

To my personal editor, Michael Ireland, thank you for your support from the beginning book proposal to the final stages of this book. I loved having your spiritual editorial skills and our long book coaching connection calls. Your spirit is contagious, and I love how some of your wordplay feedback made it into the final edits of this book.

To my incredible agent, Gareth Esersky at Carol Mann Agency, we did it! Thank you for choosing me as much as I chose you. Thank you for pitching my book with so much love. Thank you for holding the vision and spending long talks on the phone with me explaining traditional publishing. I am so grateful.

To my team at Red Wheel/Weiser and Hampton Roads, Michael, Eryn, Christine, Susie, and the RWW team, thank you for seeing the value in this book. I am thrilled to share my first book under this publishing house.

To the version of Self that cried in airport bathroom stalls preparing to live on the other side of Earth. To my earlier version of Self that dreamed to be the woman I am today. To my inner guru, for paving the path in light. Look at us now.

bibliography

Bayles, David, and Ted Orland. *Art & Fear: Observations on the Perils (and Rewards) of Artmaking.* Santa Cruz, CA: Image Continuum, 2001.

Brown, Brené. *Dare to Lead: Brave Work. Tough Conversations. Whole Hearts.* New York: Random House, 2018.

Cameron, Julia. *The Artist's Way.* New York: TarcherPerigee, 2002.

Coelho, Paulo. *The Alchemist.* San Francisco: HarperOne, 1993.

Diamant, Anita. *The Red Tent.* New York: St. Martin's, 2014.

Dyer, Wayne. *Wishes Fulfilled.* Carlsbad, CA: Hay House, 2013.

Eckert, Marcus, David D. Ebert, Dirk Lehir, Bernhard Sieland, and Matthias Berking. "Overcome Procrastination: Enhancing Emotion Regulation Skills Reduce Procrastination." *Learning and Individual Differences* 52 (December 2016): 10–18. *https://doi.org/10.1016/j.lindif.2016.10.001.*

Elkins, David. *Beyond Religion.* Wheaton, IL: Quest Books, 1998.

Frankl, Viktor. *Man's Search for Meaning: An Introduction to Logotherapy.* New York: Pocket Books, 1971.

Freud, Sigmund. *The Unconscious.* London: Penguin Books, 2005.

Goleman, Daniel. *Emotional Intelligence: Why It Can Matter More Than IQ.* New York: Bantam, 2006.

————. "What Is Emotional Self-Awareness?" Korn Ferry. May 17, 2017. *kornferry.com.*

Graff, Frank. "How Many Daily Decisions Do We Make in One Day?" PBS North Carolina. Last modified August 10, 2022. *pbsnc.org.*

Hay, Louise L. *You Can Heal Your Life.* Carlsbad, CA: Hay House, 1984.

Hoomans, Joel. "35,000 Decisions: The Great Choice of Strategic Leaders." The Leading Edge (blog), Roberts Wesleyan University. March 20, 2015. *go.roberts.edu.*

Johnson, Eric. "Art & Fear: The Ceramics Class and Quantity Before Quality." Excellent Journey (blog). March 4, 2015. *excellentjourney.net.*

Judith, Anodea. *Eastern Body, Western Mind: Psychology and the Chakra System as a Path to the Self.* Berkeley, CA: Ten Speed Press, 2011.

Karlin, David. "Mindfulness in the Workplace." *Strategic HR Review* 17, no. 2 (2018): 76–80. *https://doi.org/10.1108/SHR-11-2017-0077.*

Lamott, Anne. *Bird by Bird: Some Instructions on Writing and Life.* New York: Knopf Doubleday, 2007.

Madeson, Melissa. "Seligman's PERMA+ Model Explained: A Theory of Wellbeing." *Positive Psychology.* February 24, 2017. *positivepsychology.com.*

Makichen, Walter. *Spirit Babies: How to Communicate with the Child You're Meant to Have.* New York: Bantam Dell: 2005.

Mayyasi, Alex. "The Invention of the 'Type A' Personality." *Priceonomics.* February 16, 2016. *priceonomics.com.*

McGreevey, Sue. "Eight Weeks to a Better Brain." *The Harvard Gazette,* January 21, 2011. *news.harvard.edu.*

Miller, Lisa. *The Spiritual Child: The New Science on Parenting for Health and Lifelong Thriving.* New York: Picador Press, 2016.

Mischel, Walter, Yuichi Shoda, and Monica L. Rodriguez. "Delay of Gratification in Children." *Science* 244, no. 4907 (1989): 933–38. *https://www.science.org/doi/10.1126/science.2658056.*

Perls, Frederick S. *Gestalt Therapy Verbatim.* New York: Bantam, 1972.

Peterson, Christopher, and Martin E. P. Seligman. *Character Strengths and Virtues: A Handbook and Classification.* Washington, DC: American Psychical Association, 2004.

Petticrew, Mark P., Kelley Lee, and Martin McKee. "Type A Behavior Pattern and Coronary Heart Disease: Philip Morris's 'Crown Jewel.'" *American Journal of Public Health* 102, no. 11 (2012): 2018–25. *https://doi.org/10.2105/AJPH.2012.300816.*

Restrepo, Sandra, dir. *Brené Brown: The Call to Courage. Netflix,* 2019. *netflix.com.*

Roberts, Catherine. "The Follicular Phase: Support Your Body with the Cycle Syncing Method." Flo Living. January 10, 2022. *floliving.com.*

Rosanoff, Nancy. "PAGL." *Themetaview,* December 5, 2020. *themetaview.com.*

Roth, Geneen. *Women Food and God: An Unexpected Path to Almost Everything.* New York: Scribner, 2011.

Seligman, Martin. *Flourish: A Visionary Understanding of Happiness and Well-being.* New York: Free Press, 2011.

Seligman, Martin, and Christopher Peterson. "The VIA Character Strengths Survey." VIA Institute on Character. 2023. *viacharacter.org.*

Singer, Michael A. *The Untethered Soul: The Journey Beyond Yourself.* Oakland, CA: New Harbinger, 2007.

Strayed, Cheryl. *Dear Sugar.* Podcast audio. Accessed March 27, 2023. *wbur. org.*

Tomasulo, Dan. *Learned Hopefulness: The Power of Positivity to Overcome Depression.* Oakland, CA: New Harbinger, 2020.

Vitti, Alisa. *WomanCode: Perfect Your Cycle, Amplify Your Fertility, Supercharge Your Sex Drive, and Become a Power Source.* San Francisco: HarperOne, 2014.

Walsch, Neale Donald. *The Little Soul and the Sun.* Newburyport, MA: Hampton Roads, 1998.

Wansink, Brian, and Jeffrey Sobal. "Mindless Eating: The 200 Daily Food Decisions We Overlook." *Environment and Behavior* 39, no. 1 (2007): 106–123. *https://doi.org/10.1177/00139165062955573.*

Zahn, Roland, Jorge Moll, Mirella Paiva, Griselda Garrido, Frank Krueger, Edward D. Huey, and Jordan Grafman. "The Neural Basis of Human Social Values: Evidence from Functional MRI." *Cerebral Cortex* 19, no. 2 (2009): 276–283. *https://doi.org/10.1093/cercor/bhn080.*

about the author

Erin Rachel Doppelt is a spiritual psychology and meditation teacher with her master's in psychology in education with a spirituality mind body focus from Columbia University Teachers College. She spent her twenties living in Israel, India, and across Asia and Europe, studying with diverse gurus and yogic educators. Erin is the CEO and founder of the international brand Spiritual Intelligence, which hosts certification trainings and business and spiritual courses to support those looking to live their most unedited, nourished, and soul-authentic life. Erin is the creator of UpLevel Meditation, an active meditation framework supporting those in healing anxiety, depression, and ADD/ADHD and shifting negative thoughts toward the light. She is also the founder of the Align Coaching Certification, where you become a certified meditation teacher and spiritual psychology coach.

Erin's frameworks have been featured by SXSW, NBC, Google, Healthline, and Nike. She is also the host of *The Wise Woman Podcast*, your place to get insights on Erin's life, exciting guests, and spirituality and psychology tools to deepen your connection to Self and your highest possible timeline. She is from Chicago and enjoys traveling the world with her husband, Jon, reading in cafés, drinking strong coffee, and eating ethnic food. You can connect with her on Instagram and TikTok @erinrdoppelt or on her website, erinracheldoppelt.com. If you want to bring Erin to your yoga studio, wellness center, or corporate office, or host her for a live workshop, email her at hello@erinracheldoppelt.com.

If you desire to take the teachings in this book to the next level, apply now for the Align Coaching Certification, where you become a certified meditation teacher and spiritual psychology coach. *www.erinracheldoppelt.com /align-coaching-certification.*

If you loved this book it would mean so much to me if you could leave a review on Amazon and Good Reads as well as share it with your family and friends via word of mouth. When you leave a review, it supports the book's ranking which will help to place it in front of people who can benefit from its teachings. When you sing praises of this book and share it with aligned souls, you're giving others a possible roadmap to pursue their deepest desires and dreams. As I wrote in an early chapter, sometimes all we need is someone to place a book (like this one) on the table in front of someone who needs it. And then the miracles follow from there. Thank you so much for sharing this book with others!

To Our Readers

Hampton Roads Publishing, an imprint of Red Wheel/Weiser, publishes inspirational books from a variety of spiritual traditions and philosophical perspectives for "the evolving human spirit."

Our readers are our most important resource, and we appreciate your input, suggestions, and ideas about what you would like to see published.

Visit our website at *www.redwheelweiser.com*, where you can learn about our upcoming books and also find links to sign up for our newsletter and exclusive offers.

You can also contact us at info@rwwbooks.com or at

Red Wheel/Weiser, LLC

65 Parker Street, Suite 7

Newburyport, MA 01950